Focus on Castries St Lucia

A photo-based activity pack for primary geography

Focus on Castries St Lucia

A photo-based activity pack for primary geography

Vincent Bunce, James Foley, Wendy Morgan and Steve Scoble

THE GEOGRAPHICAL ASSOCIATION

WORLDAWARE

Acknowledgements

The authors are grateful to all the friends and colleagues in St Lucia who made the compilation of this pack possible, especially the Harvey family, the St Lucia National Trust and Mr Percy Combie. We also thank the staff of the Voluntary Services Overseas Field Office in Castries for their advice and support and the St Lucia Tourist Board, London and Castries.

The authors and publishers are also grateful to the following people and organisations for permission to reproduce copyright material:

Chris Huxley of Caribbean Images, Soufrière, St Lucia for the photographs on the centre spread, cover (St Lucian parrot), frontispiece (Gros and Petit Pitons) and page 20 of this book.

ISBN 1 899085 27 0
First published 1992; reprinted 1992, 1993, 1994, 1996 (twice).
This edition published 1997
Impression number 10 9 8 7 6 5 4 3 2 1
Year 2000 1999 1998 1997

Published by the Geographical Association, 343 Fulwood Road, Sheffield S10 3BP. The Geographical Association is a registered charity — no 313129. Worldaware is a registered charity — no 273260.

The Publications Officer of the GA would be happy to hear from other potential authors who have ideas for geography books. You may contact the Officer via the GA at the address above. The views expressed in this publication are those of the author and do not necessarily represent those of the Geographical Association or Worldaware.

Text design: Chris Hand
Cover and centre spread design: Ledgard Jepson
Illustrations: Paul Coles
Printed and bound in the UK by Kingsbury Press, Doncaster.

Contents

Introduction

This pack contains photos, background information and pupil activities which will enable a primary teacher to introduce pupils to the geography of a locality in the Caribbean. It is based on Castries, the modestly sized capital city of the tiny Commonwealth country, St Lucia.

There are 28 A4 photos which introduce a family and a school, in addition to covering the varied environments of St Lucia, including a sequence on banana farming.

Background information includes photo descriptions as well as guidance on fulfilling the requirements of the geography National Curriculum. In addition maps, information about the Harvey family, general notes about the island and a story written by Hayle Harvey are included.

There are also suggestions for activities, graded for older and younger primary pupils. These can be used as a scheme of work or can be supplemented by the use of other materials detailed in **Resources and further information** (pages 49-52).

While the pack was originally designed for key stage 2 pupils it has been used successfully in key stage 1 classes. It is very desirable that even the youngest pupils should be introduced to people and environments overseas and experience shows that photos of this kind are an ideal vehicle for developing positive images of distant places and peoples.

This revised edition includes, in addition, a colour section of information and photos. This updates the original material published in 1992, providing evidence of change in St Lucia and not least in the Harvey family.

1 Teaching about localities

National Curriculum requirements

The geography National Curriculum requires primary teachers to teach about a range of localities in the United Kingdom and in other parts of the world.

At key stage 1 the size of each locality must be equivalent to the immediate vicinity of the school, its buildings and grounds and the surrounding area within easy access.

At key stage 2 the localities are to be equivalent to a larger area than the immediate vicinity of the school and may be equated to the school's catchment area, though this is variable in size according to rural, urban or suburban location.

At key stage 1 pupils must learn about their own locality and in addition a locality whose physical and/or human features contrast with it. The contrasting locality may be in the UK or overseas.

At key stage 2 in addition to the school's own locality pupils must learn about two contrasting localities of similar size, one in the UK and the other in a country in Africa, Asia (excluding Japan), South America or Central America (including the Caribbean).

In locality studies at key stage 1 pupils should be taught:

a about the main physical and human features that give the localities their character;
b how localities may be similar and how they may differ;
c about the effects of weather on people and their surroundings;
d how land and buildings are used.

They must also become aware that the locality exists within its broader geographical context.

In locality studies at key stage 2 pupils should be taught:

a about the main physical and human features and environmental issues that give the localities their character;
b how the localities may be similar and how they may differ;
c how the features of the localities influence the nature and location of human activities within them;
d about recent or proposed changes in the localities;
e how the localities are set within a broader geographical context.

A locality in St Lucia

When choosing an overseas locality for study, you need to take all the above requirements into account. The chosen locality should not only provide adequate contrast with your school locality but must also be sufficiently well resourced to support both your pupils' thirst for knowledge and your own busy schedule.

This pack, prepared by primary geographers, is designed to enable you to teach about a particular family, attending a particular school in a named locality in St Lucia. The Harvey family live in Mon Giraud, a settlement 9km to the north of Castries, the capital city of St Lucia, and the children go to school in Castries.

Although the pack focuses on Castries, it inevitably touches on many aspects of life in other parts of the island. The Harvey family have relatives who live in other parts of the island, and make frequent visits to them. So from an early age all the Harvey children have some knowledge of the whole island which is their home. A study of the family and the school would, therefore, be incomplete if it did not draw in material concerned with life throughout the island as far as it touches upon the family and the school.

Similarities and contrasts

When introducing primary children to life in a distant place, you need to build up meaningful images of life which can be compared and contrasted with their own experience. At the same time, children should be encouraged to empathise with youngsters whose lifestyle is in some ways similar and in others dissimilar from their own. The geography National Curriculum specifies this, but many other aspects of physical, human and environmental geography can also be addressed. Opportunities for the development of mapping and other geographical skills can also be provided through a locality study. It is also possible to include content from the geographical themes: environmental quality in the case of key stage 1; weather, rivers, settlement and environmental change in key stage 2.

Using key questions

Geographical enquiry is required by the National Curriculum. In investigating places and themes, pupils should be given opportunities to:

a observe and ask questions about geographical features and issues;
b collect and record evidence to answer questions;
c analyse the evidence, draw conclusions and communicate findings.

When applied to locality study, a scheme of work guided by key geographical questions is desirable. A series of questions has been developed to help to focus study on the photographs in this pack. These questions are:

- What is it like to live in Castries?
- Why has this part of St Lucia developed in this way?
- Why is St Lucia a special place?
- How is this locality linked with other parts of St Lucia and the rest of the world?
- How is St Lucia changing and why?
- What do different people think about the changes?
- Should St Lucia be like this and what should it be like in the future?

Investigating the photographs in this pack by means of these and related questions will enable your pupils to cover the unit of National Curriculum geography which is concerned with the study of a distant locality (key stage 1) and the study of a locality in the Caribbean (key stage 2).

2 St Lucia in context

St Lucia is a small volcanic island in the Caribbean Sea, lying between Martinique and St Vincent, some 14° north of the Equator and 60° west of Greenwich (see Figure 1). It is one of a chain of islands called the Lesser Antilles. Within this chain, it is part of the Windward Islands, along with Dominica, Martinique and St Vincent.

With an area of just 616 sq km, St Lucia is quite a small island (see Figure 2). At its greatest extent it measures just 43 x 22km. It is quite mountainous compared with some neighbouring islands. Many peaks reach over 600m above sea-level, including the famous landmarks called the Pitons (Gros Piton and Petit Piton), and Mount Gimie, which reaches 958m above sea-level.

St Lucia has been settled for many centuries, first by Arawak and then by Carib Indians. The remains of their villages can be seen all over the island. The date of the first visit of people from Europe is not known with any certainty. However, St Lucia was mapped in the early sixteenth century. The first recorded written mention of the island occurs in a Spanish Royal *Cedula* — a document which divided up the New World — in 1511. The first real attempt at colonisation was made in 1605, when 67 English settlers on their way to Guiana were blown off-course and landed near Vieux Fort in the south of the island. Many died quite quickly, and the remainder fled in a Carib boat after just five weeks. The next attempt at colonisation came in 1639, when 400 English settlers arrived from Bermuda and St Kitts. They were soon killed by the Carib Indians. Then in 1651 the island was bought by the French West India Company, and an expedition of 40 French settlers arrived from Martinique. Control of St Lucia changed hands between Britain and France 14 times between 1663 and 1814 when it was finally ceded to Britain. The island remained a British colony from the early nineteenth century until 1967. St Lucia gained full independence within the British Commonwealth in February 1979.

Facts and figures

Physical geography

Area	616 sq km
Length	43km
Breadth	22km

Monthly rainfall figures for 1990 (see also Figure 5)

Total rainfall (mm)	Jan	Feb	Mar	Apr	May	Jun	Jul	Aug	Sep	Oct	Nov	Dec
Hewanorra (Vieux Fort)	142	92	25	38	134	98	126	161	163	290	84	109
Vigie (Castries)	180.6	68.7	98.2	75	125.4	164.8	190	230	210.6	597.1	107.3	146
Mahaut (rainforest)	254	277	109	120	157	180	208	239	385	533	131	126
London	71	92	17	30	4	39	7	27	25	50	22	51

Figure 1: St Lucia's location in the Caribbean

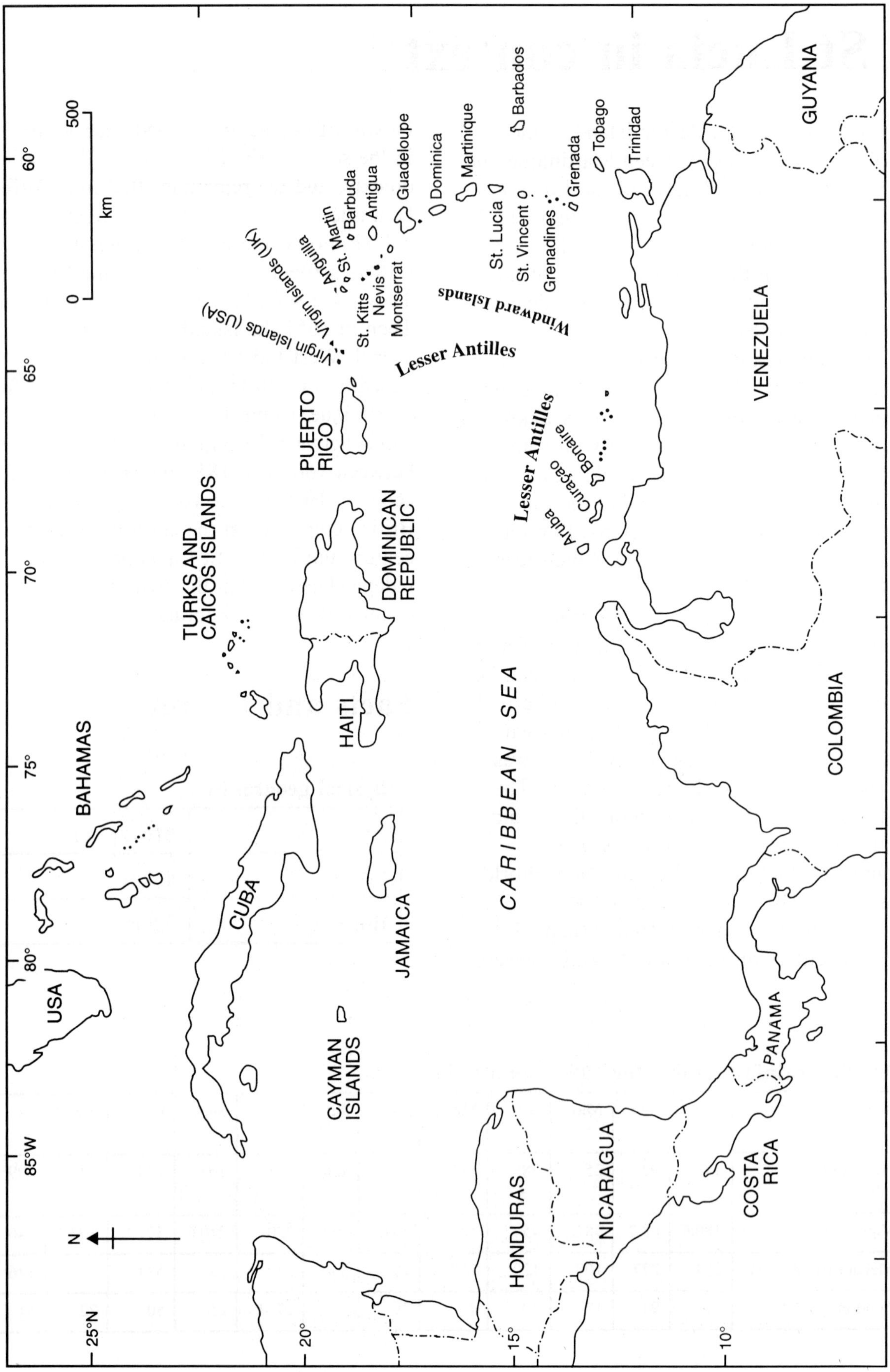

Figure 2: St Lucia settlements, surfaced roads and topography

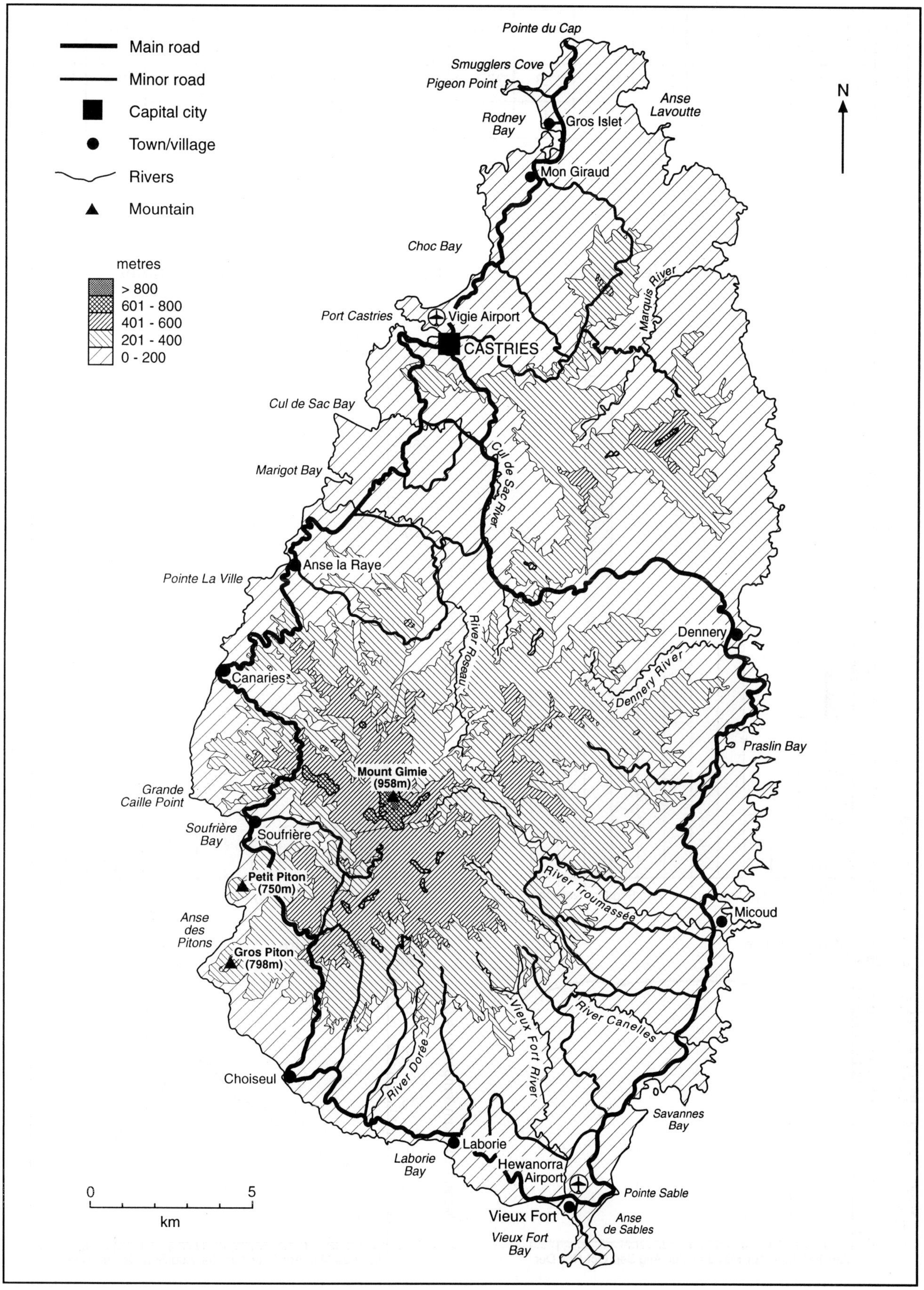

Monthly mean maximum temperature for 1990

Mean maximum temperature (°C)	Jan	Feb	Mar	Apr	May	Jun	Jul	Aug	Sep	Oct	Nov	Dec
Hewanorra	25.6	25.5	26.2	27.3	28.1	28.1	28.1	28.1	27.7	28.1	27.9	26.4
London	7.3	8.5	9.2	9.4	14.7	15.1	18.9	20.3	14.9	13.3	7.9	5.1

Figure 3: Climate graphs - Hewanorra

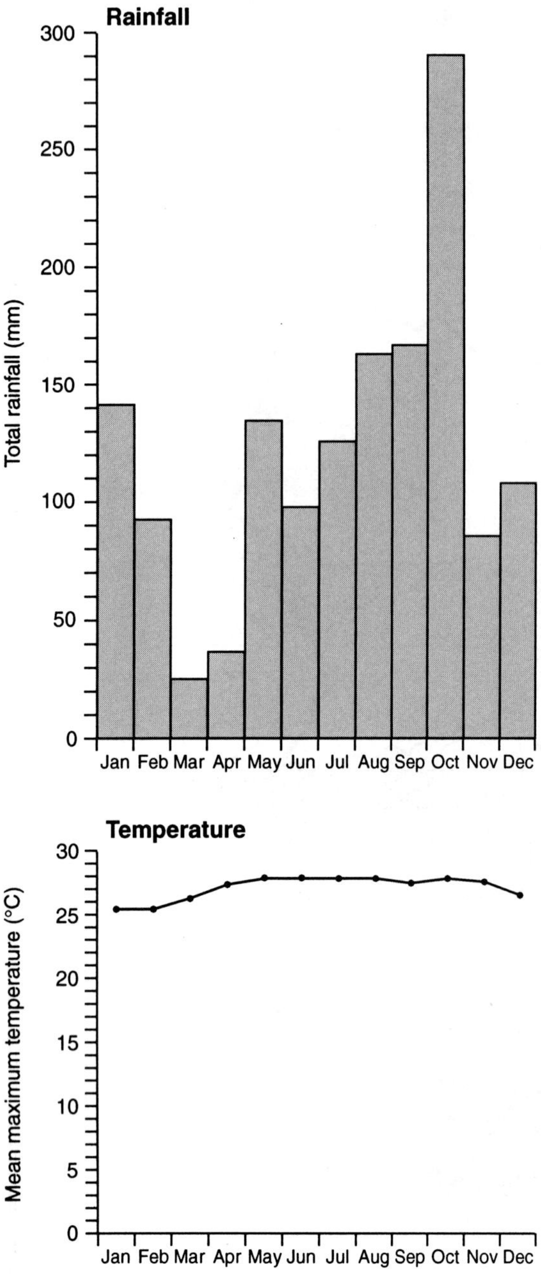

Figure 4: Climate graphs - London

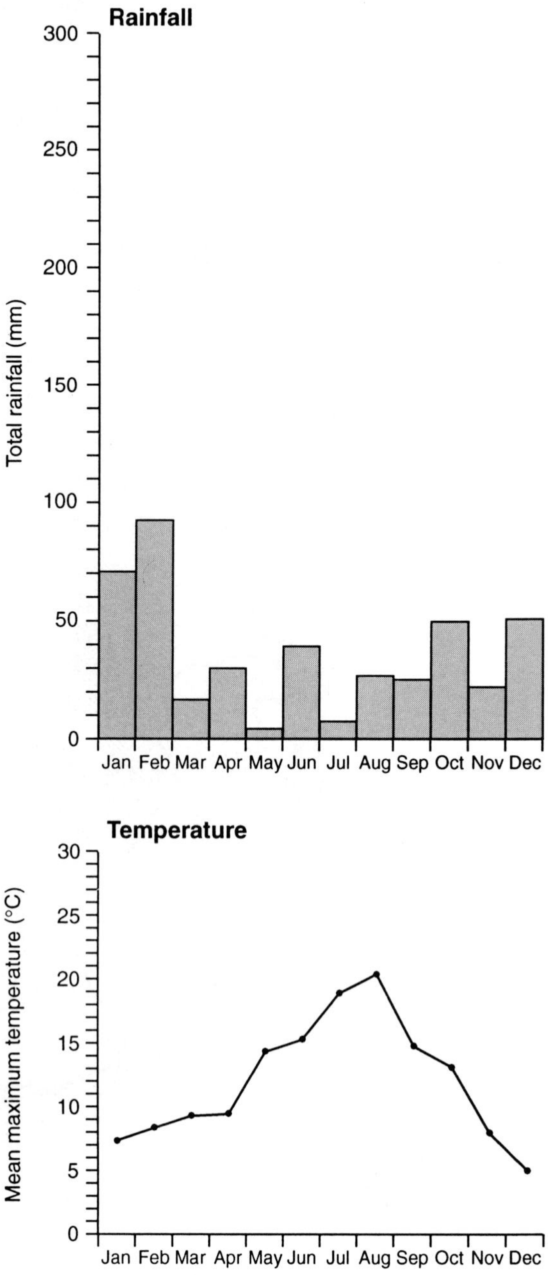

Figure 5: St Lucia rainfall, 1994

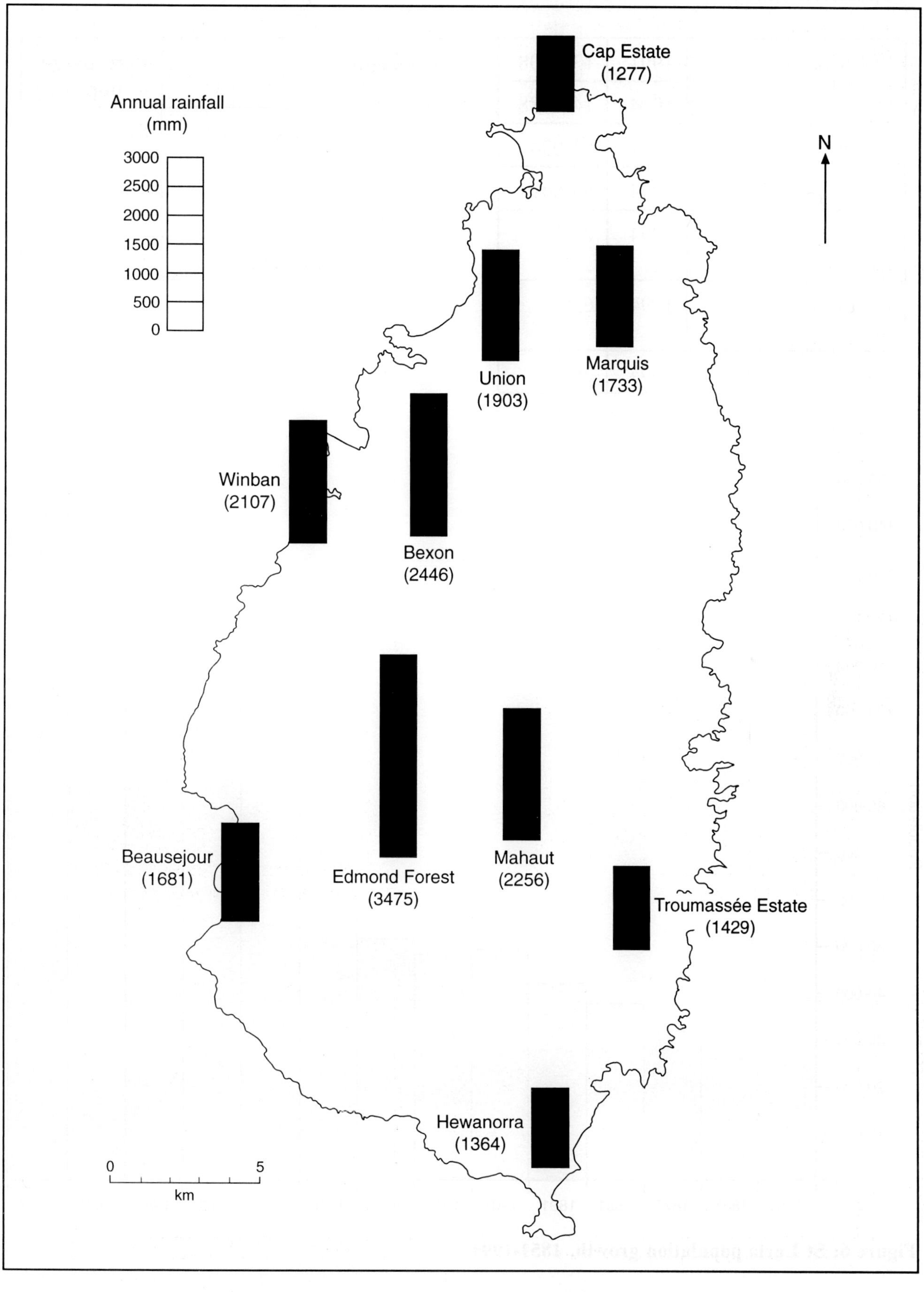

Population statistics

St Lucia	1991	133 308
	1994	142 688
Castries	1991	53 034
	1994	55 649
Birth rate per thousand	1994	24.5
Death rate per thousand	1994	6.4
Density per sq km	1994	260

Racial Composition (%)

Origin	Percentage of pop.
Black, Afro-Caribbean	87
Mixed	9
Indian	3
Other (including white)	1

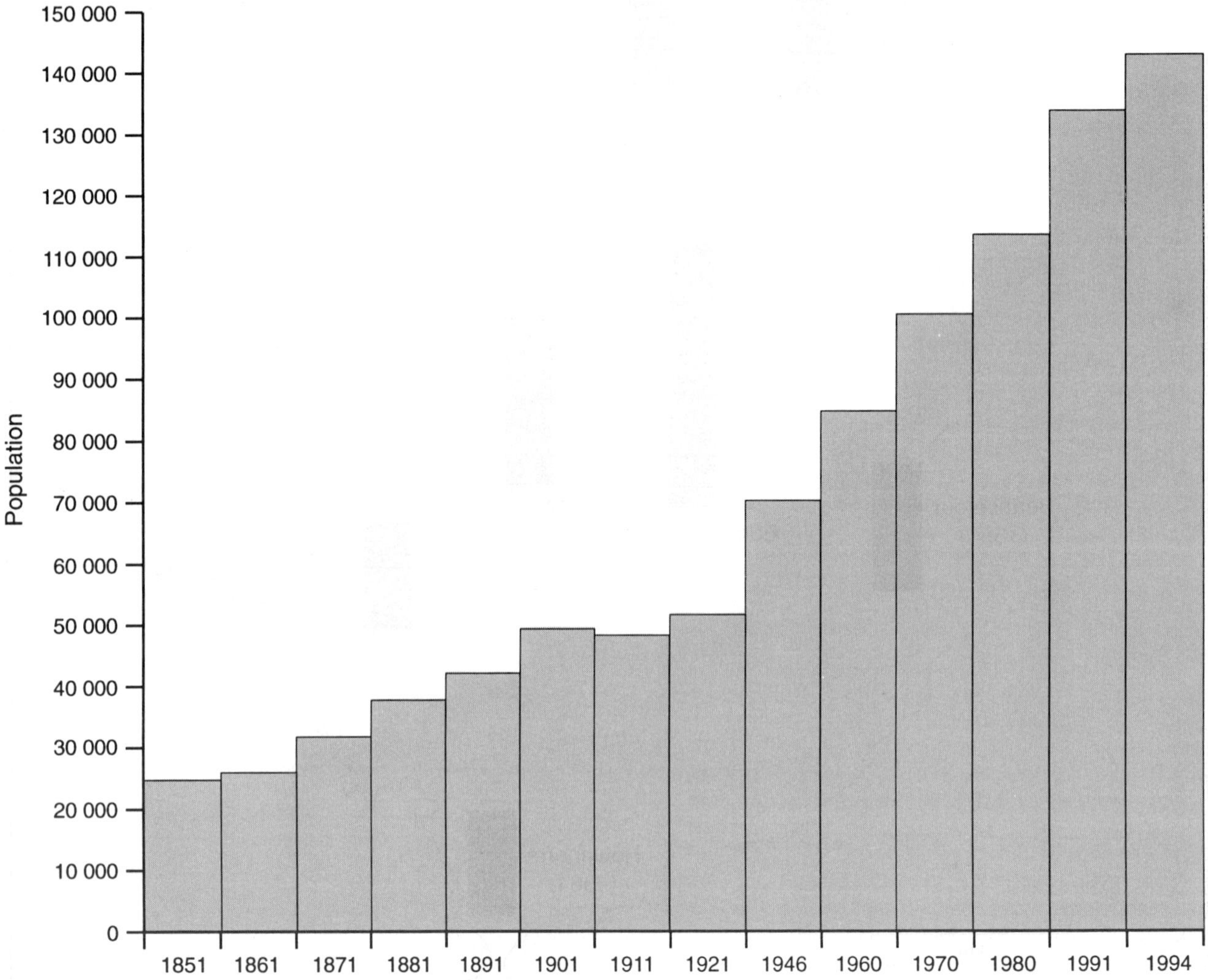

Figure 6: St Lucia population growth, 1851-1994

Figure 7: Population density, by region, 1993

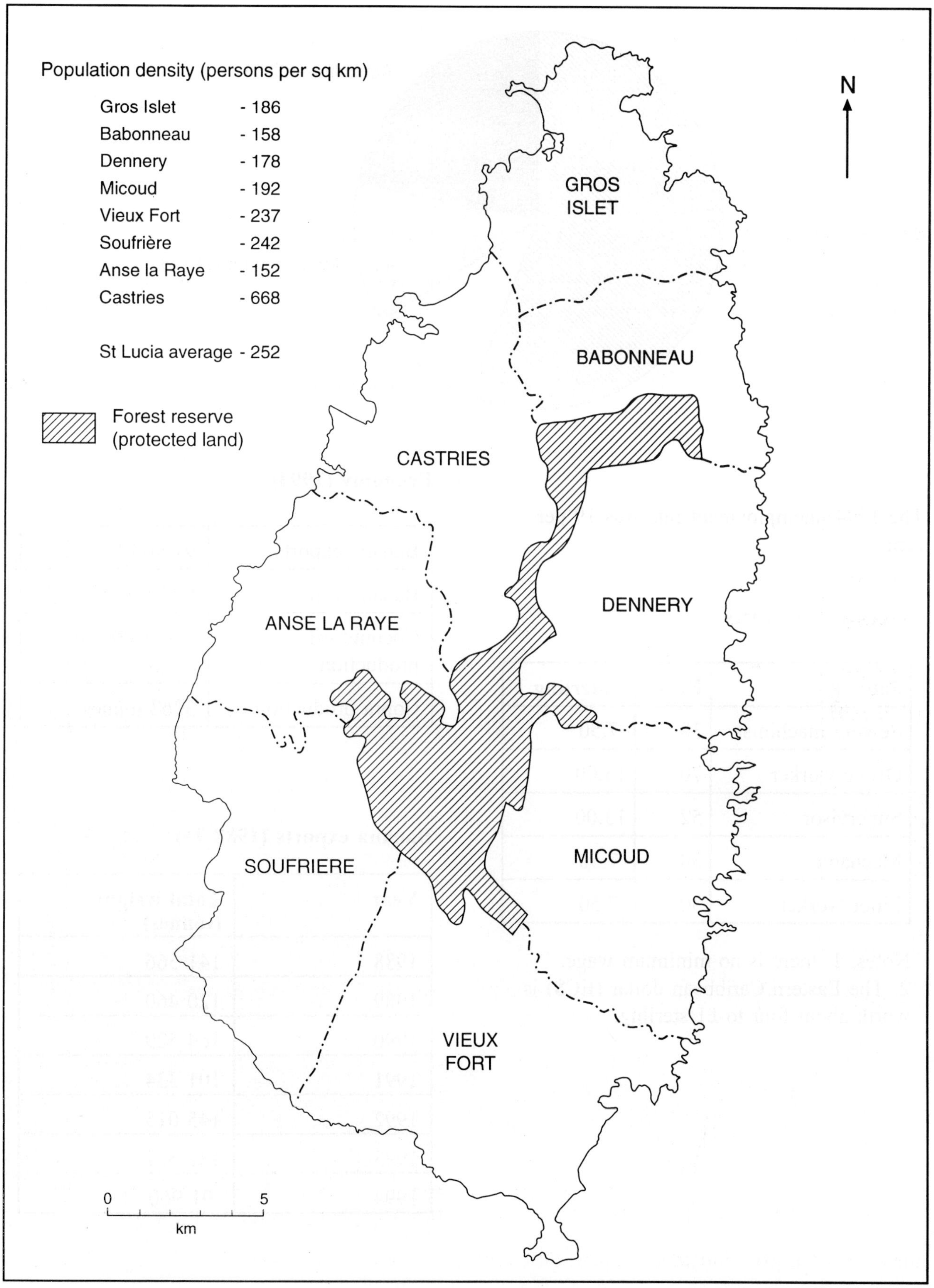

Figure 8: Employment structure, 1991 (percentage by sector)

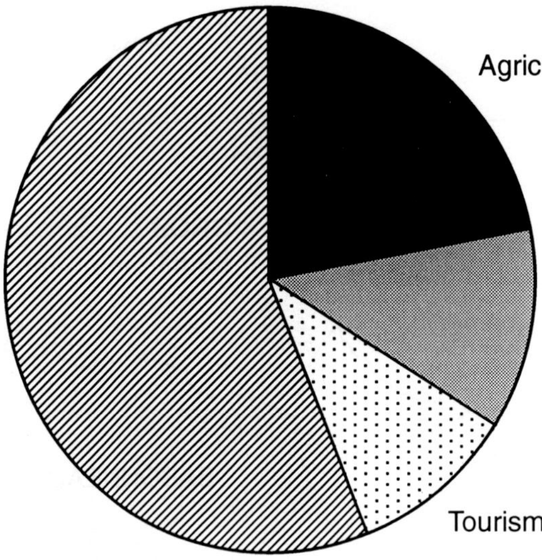

The 1994 unemployment rate was 19 per cent.

Weekly wage rates[1]

Job	EC$[2]	£ sterling
Sewing machinist	30	7.50
Office worker	70	15.00
Supervisor	52	13.00
Mechanic	30	7.50
Floor worker	30	7.50

Notes: 1. there is no minimum wage.
2. The Eastern Caribbean dollar (EC$) is worth about four to £1 sterling.

Economy (1994)

Banana exports	91 960 tonnes
Banana value	US$126 409
Coconut oil production	2 124 000 litres
Copra production	3262 tonnes

Banana exports (1988-94)

Year	Total weight (tonnes)
1988	141 566
1989	120 460
1990	164 529
1991	101 334
1992	145 015
1993	132 537
1994	91 960

Figure 9: Land use in St Lucia

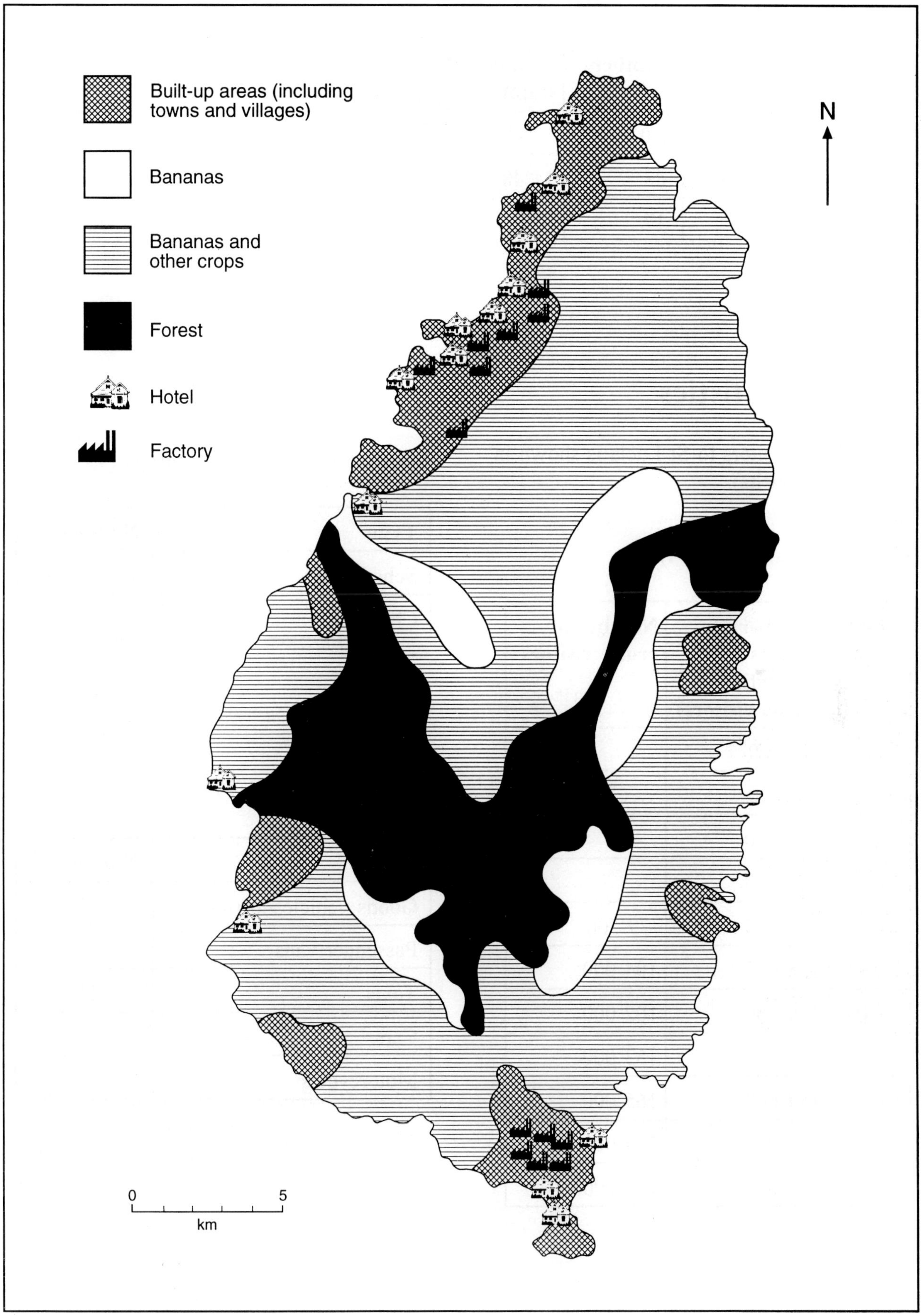

Education (1993-94)

Type of school	Number	Number of pupils	Number of teachers
Pre-school	150	7114	402
Primary	88	31 487	1105 (687 trained, 418 untrained)
Secondary	17	9721	446 (218 graduate, 228 non-graduate)

Tourism statistics

The origin of visitors to St Lucia is shown in Figure 10 (opposite).

Visitor arrivals (1984-94)

Year	Number of visitors (excluding cruise visitors)	Number of cruise visitors
1984	89 900	-
1985	96 600	-
1986	115 000	-
1987	127 000	-
1988	133 000	79 500
1989	138 000	104 000
1990	149 000	102 000
1991	166 000	153 000
1992	184 000	165 000
1993	201 000	154 000
1994	224 000	172 000

International aircraft landings (1994)

Type	Number
Scheduled	19 751
Charter	8570

Transport figures (1994)

Type	Number
Goods vehicles/lorries	13 517
Passenger vans	4173
Taxis	1941
Cars	9149
Motorcycles	898

Figure 10: Origin of visitors, 1994

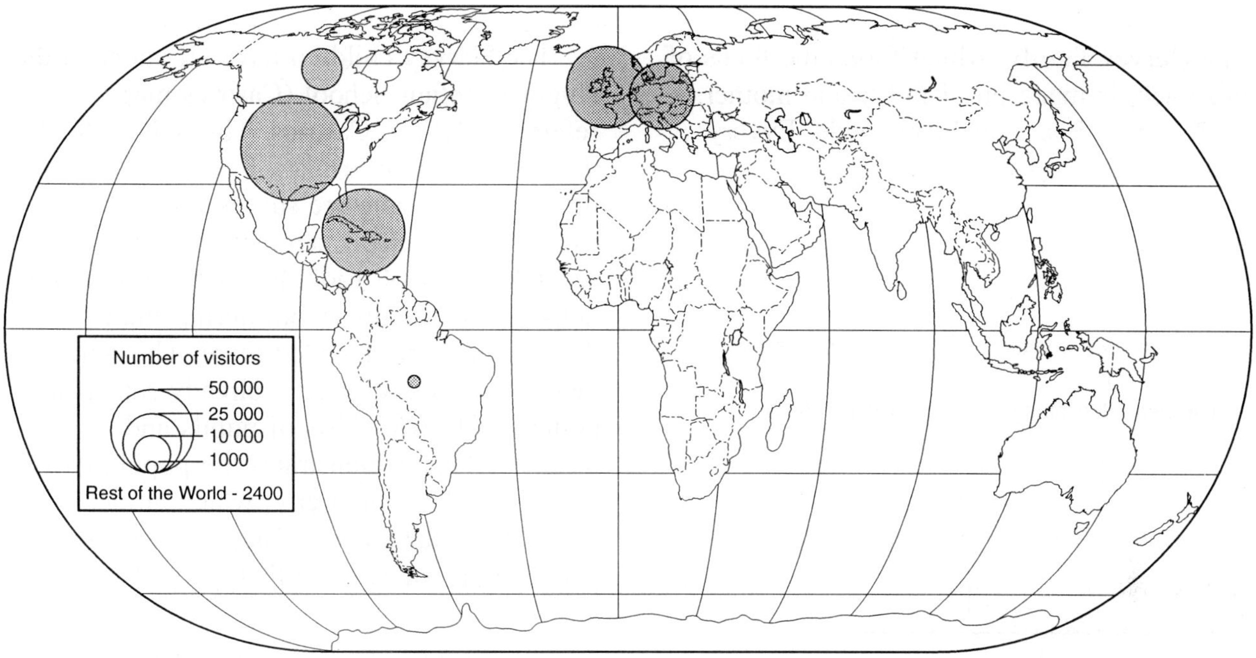

Origin of visitors, 1994

Caribbean	51 000
UK	47 000
Rest of Europe	31 000
USA	78 000
Canada	12 000
Latin America	1200
Rest of World	2400

3 The Harvey family and Castries

The Harvey family, which forms the focus of this pack, is made up of father and mother, Rawle and Liola, daughters Hayle, Evvery and Thia and son Gimel.

Emmanuel Joyeux m Carmen Charlemagne — Everton Harvey m Eileen Harvey

Liola Joyeux m Rawle Harvey

Hayle | Evvery | Thia | Gimel

Figure 11: The Harvey family tree

The Harvey children have all attended the Anglican Infant School (Castries map reference: K5) in Castries. This school feeds the Canon Laurie Primary School, after which those children who are successful in the Common Entrance Examination move to secondary school. Liola has been a voluntary helper at the infant school during the time that her children attended there. The school is heavily oversubscribed. It already runs a shift system, with two shifts of pupils and teachers. This demonstrates the popularity of schools in the capital city, which attract pupils from far afield. Education here is perceived as superior to that in rural areas.

Castries

The Harvey family live adjacent to the main road north of the capital, Castries, in a small settlement called Mon Giraud. However, their

The Harvey family relaxing in their garden, May 1996. Photo: © Chris Huxley

daily lives are centred firmly on Castries. It is in the capital that they go to school, church and shop. Rawle Harvey's work servicing refrigerators and air conditioning units takes him all over the island.

Castries, with its population of over 55 000 (almost one-third of St Lucia's total), is a busy city located on the northwest coast. As well as being the capital city, with government offices, a cathedral, shops, a large market and the headquarters of many companies and newspapers, its harbour makes it a good port.

During its history, the city has suffered many setbacks, including damage from four serious fires and from hurricanes. Much of the city centre was destroyed by a fire in 1948, after which it was rebuilt along modern, planned lines with a grid-iron pattern of streets. There is evidence, both in building styles and in street names, of St Lucia's dual English and French heritage (its ownership passed between the two colonial powers 14 times).

As well as a large harbour with a berth for large passenger cruise liners, Castries has a newly constructed duty-free complex at Point Seraphine. This is connected to the commercial centre of the town by the John Compton Highway (named after the island's former Prime Minister). New government buildings on the waterfront are another recent addition to the city's skyline, as is the new fruit and vegetable market. The capital also has its own airport at Vigie. The city is surrounded by high land, including Morne Fortune (the 'Hill of good luck'), which give it a distinctive appearance. Many of the older buildings were destroyed in fires and hurricanes, but the Cathedral of the Immaculate Conception dates from 1897, and in Derek Walcott Square, named after the St Lucian poet and Nobel Prize winner, is a 400 year-old saman tree.

4 Growing up in Castries
by Hayle Harvey (written at age 17)

Vigie was lovely! We lived in Daddy's 'bachelor house' as Mom called it. It had one bedroom, living room, dining area, kitchen, and a bathroom. Dad's workshop and office were next to the house. He was a refrigeration technician and a private pilot, and Mom was a housewife. We had a beautiful panoramic view of the John Compton Highway and the Castries Harbour.

There were many types of flowers around our home, especially exoras, marigold, hibiscus, and roses. The area was peaceful and quiet, despite that there were not many children to play with, I loved it.

My school was about five minutes' walk away from home and Dad brought me to school every morning. It was a private school and the owner Mrs Lake managed it on her own, in the privacy of her own home.

Going to school was always fun and I looked forward to each new day. Mrs Lake played the piano while we sang our favourite

A pre-school in Castries

View of Castries Harbour looking north towards Vigie

song, 'Jesus loves the little children', which we sang almost every day. She also taught us to read and write and always told us that learning to read and write were the greatest things that we could learn in the world. 'All work and no play makes Jack a dull boy!' Mrs Lake always said. We played games, made paper dolls' furniture from matchboxes, all with the help of Mrs Lake.

A few weeks before school closed for Christmas holidays, we would prepare for the Annual Christmas Show. At the show everything went just as planned, and afterwards, we had a party which was attended by parents and children.

My holidays were spent shopping, visiting Aunt Betty, going down to the Reef which was the marina, and going to the beach.

We would climb to the flat roof top, at Aunt Betty's, and there we had an even more fantastic view of the John Compton Highway and the Castries Harbour, as well as Morne Fortune. Sometimes my Uncle Cletus would bring his video camera along and tape our activities such as posing for pictures and pretending to have little shows.

The marina at Rodney Bay

Reduit Beach

Castries Harbour from the Morne

On weekends we usually travelled to Laborie and Choiseul, which were two villages in the south of the island, to visit my grandparents. My grandfather and his wife, who is my step-grandmother, always enjoyed it whenever we went to visit them in Laborie. I enjoyed every moment. We usually went for walks, since visiting old friends and relatives in the village and that was always fun, since I met someone new almost every time.

In Choiseul, we visited my grandmother and that was always exciting. I loved going to watch the rabbits, the pigs, and the chickens. Granny also had guinea pigs which ran all over the place and I always attempted to catch them but it was virtually impossible. My Uncle Mikey always succeeded and he would let me hold it and that was fun.

During the holidays, we also went flying around the island in Dad's small plane. That was definitely exciting. I enjoyed visiting Dad's parents in Barbados. Whenever Dad took Mom and me on these trips, I saw the fantastic Twin Peaks (the Pitons) and the Sulphur Springs in Soufrière. Usually Dad flew directly over our home and it was fun to see our home from above.

Time went by and soon I had a little sister. Her name was Evvery and she was very troublesome. She began to enjoy all the fun that I had on weekends, when I was the only child. We had lots of fun together, picking cherries, helping Mom plant flowers, vegetables and fruits in her kitchen garden.

I always enjoyed helping Mom in her kitchen garden. She had pawpaw, oranges, grapefruits, mangoes, tamarind, cherry and a host of others. She also planted chive, carrots, parsley, celery, lettuce and Chinese cabbage.

It was not long before Mom told me that we were moving to Gros Islet, which is in the north of the island. I do not really remember what my reaction to the idea was, but one thing I do know is that I really do miss Vigie. One afternoon, when we returned from seeing the house which was just being

Evvery's plan of the house at Gros Islet

View of St Lucia looking north from the most southerly point on the island

constructed, I went into Mom's bedroom and saw all Mom's belonging scattered on her bed. I called her, she realised that we had been robbed. My favourite necklace was stolen, as well as Mom's coin collection, jewellery, and perfume.

In December 1979, we moved to Gros Islet. The house was really nice. It had four bedrooms, two bathrooms, a kitchen, a living room, dining area and a fairly big balcony.

The area in which we lived was fairly quiet and we had a nice view of the Gros Islet Highway and the tallest hill in St Lucia which is Morne Fortune which means 'Hill of good luck'. (Mount Gimie is actually the highest hill at 958m — Editor's note.)

On the night of August 12, 1980, St Lucia was hit by Hurricane Allen. The house was lit by candles, since there was a power failure. It was raining heavily, accompanied by lightning, thunder and strong winds.

During the night, Aunt Cynthia observed that the roof of the house was blown off when she went to the bathroom. Dad said that we would go to the St Lucian Hotel for safety. Unfortunately we were unable to go down the driveway since there was a big tree lying across the road. Dad attempted to push the tree aside with the aid of the van, but it was of no use. The tree was much too big. We went to a neighbour's house and while there I felt a lot safer. I tried to sleep but I could not. The wind, which was howling, sounded like the 'Incredible Hulk' when he was angry.

The following day we returned home and I went to see where the roof had landed. It fitted itself quite perfectly in Mom's kitchen garden. Repairs began on the house immediately and gradually everything was back to normal.

In 1981, I had a new born baby sister and her name was Thia. She was quite pretty and as time went by she certainly got brave. She did not exactly learn to walk, but suddenly one afternoon, she just got up and took one step and fell down. She tried again, until she succeeded in walking three steps, and she continued to walk since then.

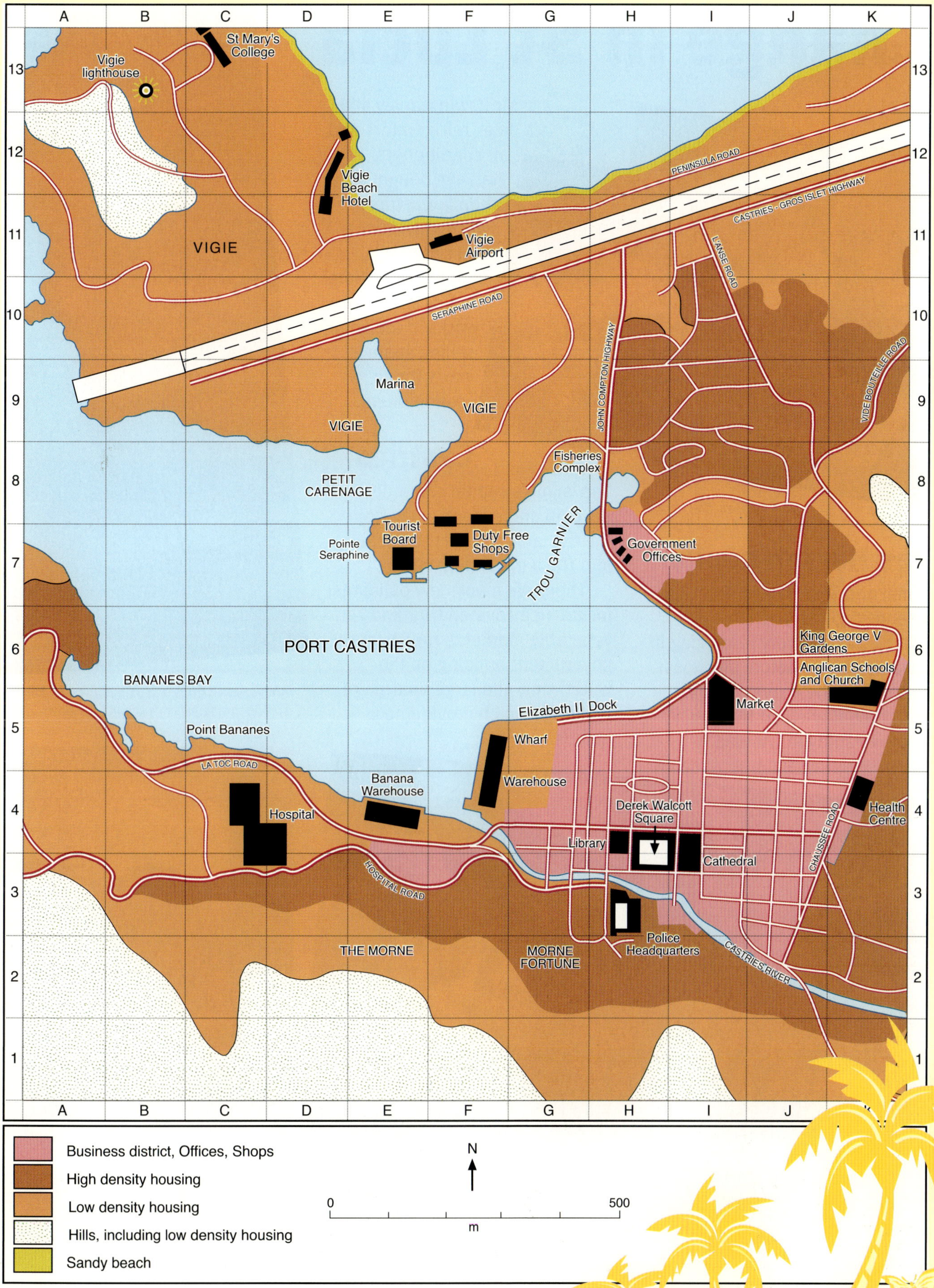
A B C D E F G H I J K
13 12 11 10 9 8 7 6 5 4 3 2 1
St Mary's College
Vigie lighthouse
Vigie Beach Hotel
VIGIE
Vigie Airport
PENINSULA ROAD
CASTRIES - GROS ISLET HIGHWAY
L'ANSE ROAD
SERAPHINE ROAD
JOHN COMPTON HIGHWAY
VIDE BOUTEILLE ROAD
Marina
VIGIE
VIGIE
PETIT CARENAGE
Fisheries Complex
Tourist Board
Duty Free Shops
Pointe Seraphine
TROU GARNIER
Government Offices
PORT CASTRIES
King George V Gardens
Anglican Schools and Church
BANANES BAY
Market
Elizabeth II Dock
Point Bananes
Wharf
LA TOC ROAD
Warehouse
Banana Warehouse
Hospital
Derek Walcott Square
Health Centre
CHAUSSEE ROAD
Library
Cathedral
HOSPITAL ROAD
Police Headquarters
THE MORNE
MORNE FORTUNE
CASTRIES RIVER
Business district, Offices, Shops
High density housing
Low density housing
Hills, including low density housing
Sandy beach
N
0
500
m

Castries

Change in St Lucia

Above: The Harvey family at dinner

The Harvey family

Gimel and Thia Harvey now attend secondary schools in Castries, and Evvery is working in a travel agency before she goes to college. The Harveys' eldest daughter, Hayle, left the family home to study in Trinidad.

Mr Rawle Harvey still fixes refrigerators and air conditioners. The Harveys bought a shop in Castries, which Rawle uses as a base for supplies. Mrs Liola Harvey sometimes works in the shop selling spare parts for air conditioners.

Castries

The island's capital continues to develop and expand away from the flat land around the port up into the surrounding hills.

There are many new buildings, including a covered fruit and vegetable market, a fourth large government building on the waterfront, and large apartment buildings which provide new homes.

Above: As Castries gets bigger, new buildings spread up the hillsides around the town

Above: The market in Castries. This man is selling wicker furniture, straw hats and sandals

Above: Tropical storm Debbie caused this damage at Soufrière in 1994

The island

The island has also developed and changed. Tropical storm Debbie devastated the island in 1994. Many rivers overflowed, and some bridges were washed away.

Although bananas are still widely grown, they provide a living for fewer people than in the past. It costs a lot to grow bananas on the small farms in St Lucia, so it is difficult to compete with other countries where bananas are grown more cheaply on large plantations.

Many St Lucians are looking for other sources of income. The number of factories in St Lucia is steadily growing, and the island is also attracting more and more visitors. New hotels are being built for them. The island's roads and other facilities continue to be improved.

Above: The Windjammer Landing Beach Resort is typical of the luxurious tourist development taking place in St Lucia

Above: This is the new Windward and Leeward Brewery in St Lucia

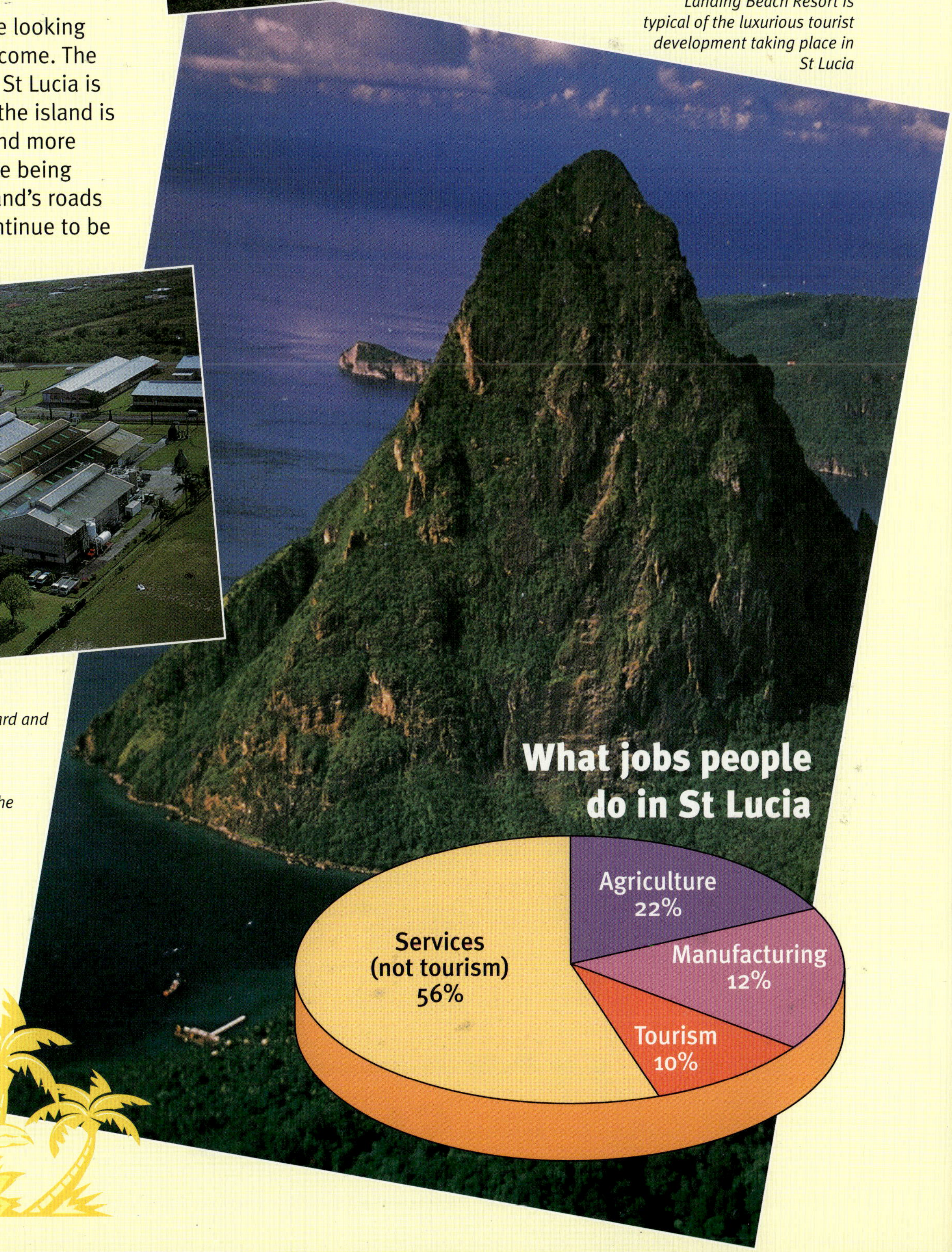

Right: One of the Pitons, twin landmarks of St Lucia: this is the Petit Piton

Pointe du Cap
Smugglers Cove
Pigeon Point
Anse Lavoutte
Rodney Bay
Gros Islet
Mon Giraud
Main road
Minor road
Capital city
Town/village
Rivers
Mountain
N
Choc Bay
Marquis River
metres
> 800
601 - 800
401 - 600
201 - 400
0 - 200
Port Castries
Vigie Airport
CASTRIES
Cul de Sac Bay
Cul de Sac River
Marigot Bay
Anse la Raye
Pointe La Ville
River Roseau
Dennery
Canaries
Dennery River
Praslin Bay
Mount Gimie (958m)
Grande Caille Point
Soufrière Bay
Soufrière
Petit Piton (750m)
River Troumassée
Micoud
Anse des Pitons
Gros Piton (798m)
River Canelles
Vieux Fort River
River Dorée
Choiseul
Savannes Bay
Laborie
Laborie Bay
Hewanorra Airport
Pointe Sable
0
5
km
Vieux Fort
Anse de Sables
Vieux Fort Bay

St Lucia

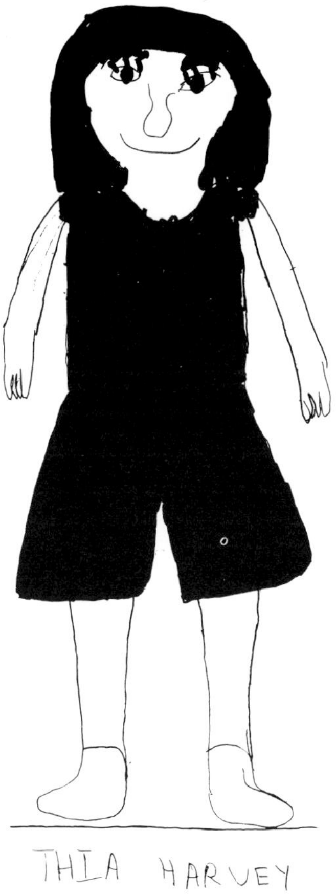

Self portrait of Thia (aged 10)

Self portrait of Gimel (aged 8)

In 1982, I had a new born baby brother and he was named Gimel. My cousin Robert came home from the hospital telling Evvery, Thia and me, that Mom just had the ugliest baby ever. When Mom arrived home a few days letter, we saw that Gimel was very cute. It was great to have a little brother, since I had two sisters already.

The following year Evvery and I made our First Communion in Laborie. That day was very special. We had white dresses with veils which made us look like little brides, and the boys were dressed in three piece suits. Mom, Granny, Granddad, Granny, Aunt Elsa, Aunt Deborah and Greatgran all went to Church with us. It was a wonderful day and it was the first time that we would be receiving the 'Body of Christ' or the Holy Eucharist as it is called in the Roman Catholic Church.

After the Church service, we went to my Grandparent's home and we had the traditional lunch which comprised Pumpkin Soup, with our families and friends. In the afternoon we had a party which was especially for Evvery, my youngest Aunt, Sinette, and me. We danced not only with our friends, but with Mom, Granddad, most of our Aunts and Uncles and Greatgran.

Growing up in Castries also meant that we attended local events and festivals, such as Carnival, the Carol Festival and Aqua Action. Carnival was usually held four days before the Lenten Season. Carnival was always exciting, because there were many brightly coloured costumes and exciting music, and we looked forward to it every year.

The Carol Festival was always a pleasure to go to. It was held around Christmas time and different choirs from around the island performed. My favourite choir was Bel Canto.

Aqua Action was lots of excitement and it was held over the Whitsuntide Weekend. It was a weekend filled with sporting activities – volleyball, water skiing, windsurfing, long distance marathons and lots more. It was usually held at Pigeon Point in the north of the Island.

At the St Joseph's Convent Secondary School, which I attended, we celebrated local events and festivals, such as National Day, the Feast of Mary which was held in May and the Patron Saint of our school which was held in March. We celebrated these events and festivals by staging inter-house competitions for Art, Drama, Dance and Song.

I graduated from the St Joseph's Convent in 1991, at the age of seventeen. We had a wonderful graduation ceremony, which was attended by my entire family, my Aunt Phillipa, Uncle Jacques, and my best friends, Lailah and Stephen.

Thia's drawing of her family

5 The photos explained

The photos have been grouped into three sections. The first features the Harvey family and their activities, the second examines the numerous contrasting environments in and around Castries and the third illustrates agriculture, particularly banana farming in St Lucia. Figures 12 and 13 show the location of the photos.

These photos were taken in 1991, since when many changes have inevitably occurred. Geography is a dynamic subject and consideration of change a positive feature of the National Curriculum. Information about these changes is contained in the colour section (stapled into the centre of this book), which will enable teachers to emphasise changes that have affected the Harvey family in particular and St Lucia generally.

Growing up in Castries, St Lucia

Photo 1: The Harvey Family in their garden

The family can be seen dressed in their 'Sunday best' all ready to drive into Castries. There they will join with friends for mass in one of the city's Catholic churches. On special feast days, the family attend mass at the Cathedral of the Immaculate Conception.

The Harvey's single storey house, seen in the rear of the photo with a galvanised iron roof, is unusual in having a large garden surrounding it.

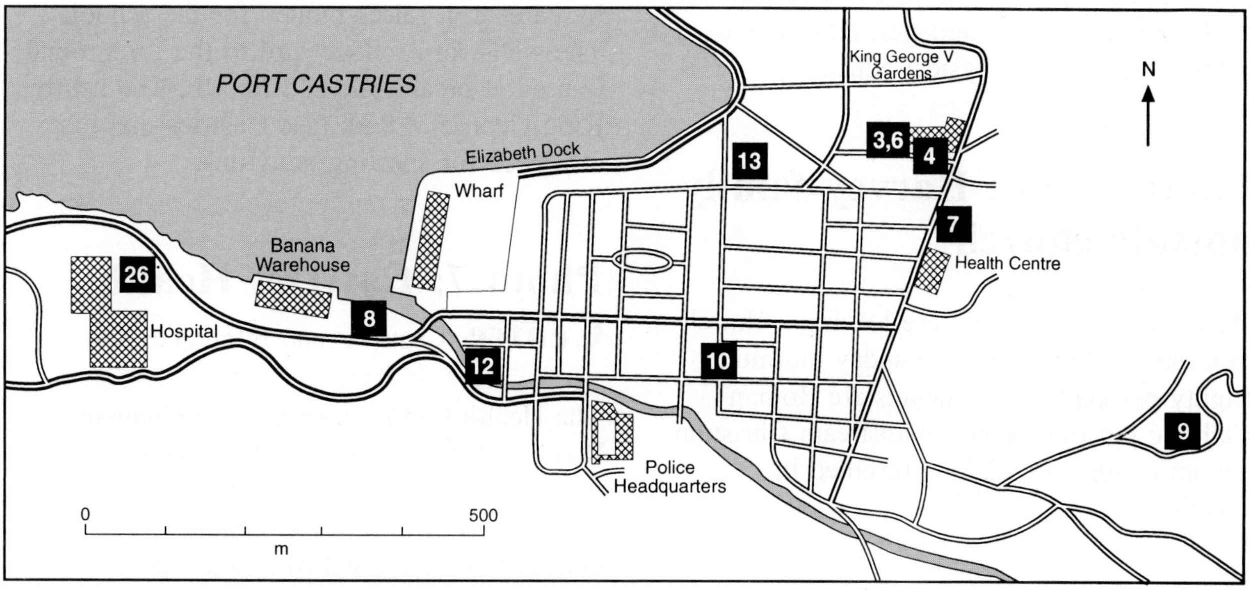

Figure 12: Location of photos in Castries

Photo 2: Thia and Evvery going to school

The two girls, Thia (right) and Evvery (left) are dressed in their uniforms and are ready to set off to school. Their father, Rawle Harvey, drives the children to school. Their brother Gimel attends the Anglican Infant School, and Thia the nearby Canon Laurie Primary School, while Evvery is a pupil at St Joseph's Convent Secondary School. The Harvey family live near the main road which leads south into Castries, where the children all go to school.

Photo 3: Inside the Anglican Infant School, Castries

(Castries map reference: K5)

A class can be seen at work on the school's upper storey, where five classes adjoin each other, blackboards and bookcases divide them. The school has 673 children (aged 5-9 years) in 19 classes. There are 19 teachers and the headteacher, Mrs Daphne James. Normally the children would transfer to Canon Laurie Primary School at 7, but overcrowding prevents this. The children study mathematics, languages, arts, social studies, health and physical education.

Photo 4: The Harvey family outside church

Here the Harvey family are leaving a church in Castries after mass on Sunday morning. Eighty per cent of St Lucians are Roman Catholic but most other mainstream Christian denominations are also represented in Castries.

Photo 5: Thia Harvey

Ten-year-old Thia relaxes in the living room of the family home in Gros Islet. Hayle describes her impressions of the house when they moved in 1979:

> 'The house was really nice. It had four bedrooms, two bathrooms, a kitchen, a living room, dining room, and a fairly big balcony. The area in which we lived was fairly quiet and we had a nice view of the Gros Islet Highway and Morne Fortune, which means 'Hill of good luck'.'

A plan of the house can be found on page 25.

Photo 6: The Anglican Infant School, exterior

(Castries map reference: K5)

This two-storey school has open air walkways alongside the classrooms. There are no glass windows, but protection from the sun is provided by venetian blinds. Open-fronted cupboards under the balcony allow storage for lunch boxes and school bags. The new building on the right is the tuck shop, staffed by parents, it raises money for the school. The well-worn school yard in the foreground is used at break time and for PE. The nearby King George V Park (see Castries map) is also used for sporting activities.

Photo 7: Castries Health Centre (Castries map reference: K4)

The Health Centre is situated in Chaussée Road on the eastern side of Castries, close to the Anglican Primary Schools. This enables easy access in times of emergency. The construction is typical of much recent building in Castries, with wood, stone and concrete being used. Minibuses wait nearby providing a service for those patients without their own transport. Many people will have come in from the surrounding rural areas. Nurses wearing white uniforms with coloured belts can be seen.

Environments

Photo 8: Castries waterside

(Castries map: F4-F5)

St Lucia's capital city, Castries, sprawls around an almost landlocked harbour, surrounded by hills. In the foreground is the container handling area which can accommodate cargo ships and fishing vessels. Elsewhere is a berth for large passenger liners. The three modern buildings on the waterfront at the rear of the photo are government buildings, which house various ministries, and the Prime Minister's office.

Photo 9: Houses in Castries

This is a group of houses on the southern side of Castries harbour. The wood and galvanised iron construction of the buildings is typical of many houses in the capital, though some make use of cement and plaster-board. The wires carrying electricity to the houses can be seen. The pitched roofs and floors raised on stilts are features to cope with tropical rains. Window-blinds can also be seen – giving protection from the sun.

Photo 10: Peynier Street

(Castries map reference: I3)

This photo was taken facing south. The proximity of the surrounding hillsides to the capital can be seen here, with a substantial amount of housing developed on fairly steep slopes affording good views. The lush vegetation is a result of the moist tropical climate. The deep open gutter to the right of the steeply cambered road is also related to the area's climate. Features to note include the Central Bakery at the end of the street, and the British influence on the city, as evidenced by the familiar street signs.

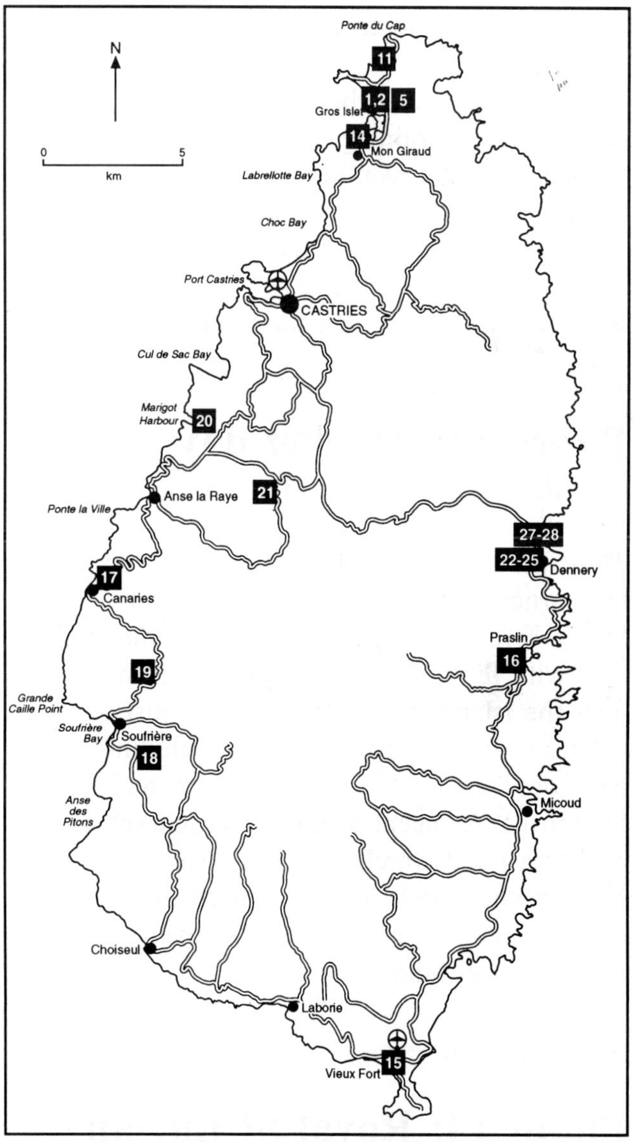

Figure 13: Location of photos around St Lucia

Photo 11: Housing on Cap Estate

To the north of Castries is an area of more expensive housing occupied by some of the island's better-off residents. This house, again built into a hillside, has stunning views south over the north-western coastal lowlands of the island. The vegetation is again lush and includes hibiscus and bougainvillaea.

Photo 12: The Castries river

(Castries map reference: G3, H3, etc.)

The Castries river, which flows through the capital before draining into the bay at Pointe Bananes, can be seen here about 500m from the sea. The river bed is littered with rubbish which has been dumped there. The houses which line one bank have sewage outlets which open directly into the river.

Photo 13: Market day

(Castries map reference: I5)

The fruit and vegetable market is located at the corner of Jermie Street and Peynier Street. Every Saturday the market comes to life, with farmers bringing produce from all over the island to sell. Bananas are just one of many products for sale here, including: mangoes, pineapple, melon, coconut and breadfruit. Adjacent to this street market, in an iron-roofed warehouse, is a covered market which sells domestic items like coconut matting, pottery, pans, woven materials and other textiles.

Photo 14: Royal St Lucian

The Royal St Lucian Hotel is one of the island's newest. Located north of Castries on Reduit beach, it opened in December 1990. The man pictured is one of the hotel receptionists. Among the facilities are a swimming pool with swim-up bar, disco, five-star service and cuisine. The hotel opens directly onto the beach. Its grounds have been extensively landscaped. Tourism earned St Lucia US$151 million in 1990 (10 per cent of Gross Domestic Product).

Photo 15: Cariman Electronics, Vieux Fort

Among the types of employment available on the island is industrial work. Cariman Electronics manufacture resistors and thermistors for their American parent company, in a free trade zone in the south of the island. There are 224 workers, mostly young female. Locating in the free trade zone has brought many financial advantages to Cariman – low cost factory space, duty-free entry and exit for raw materials and equipment, a 15-year tax 'holiday' and minimum customs formalities. Industries such are encouraged to come to St Lucia by the National Development Corporation.

Photo 16: Boat-building at Praslin

Praslin is a small community located on the island's east coast. A proportion of the local people rely on fishing as a livelihood. On this sheltered beach traditional boat-building skills are used to hollow out the gommier tree. The project is funded by a co-operative and by the St Lucia National Trust. Once the trunks have been hollowed and treated with water and fire to make them watertight, the sides are built up, and an outboard motor fitted.

Photo 17: The West Coast road near Canaries

St Lucia is small enough to have a simple road network. One main road links all the settlements located around the coast. The quality of the road surface varies enormously.

In parts (from Castries to Anse la Raye), where money has been provided by the British Government's overseas aid budget, the road is properly surfaced. Elsewhere, as shown here (near Canaries), the surface has cracked and is often pot-holed. This is partly due to the rigours of the tropical climate with its heavy rains and high temperatures. The volume and variety of traffic using the often narrow and winding road also makes it difficult to maintain effectively.

Photo 18: Volcanic landscape at Soufrière

While St Lucia's environment mostly consists of rainforest, one area near Soufrière still demonstrates its volcanic origin. The Sulphur Springs are a key tourist attraction. This 10ha site is technically volcanically active though the complex geology means that lava is no longer emitted. Nearby are hot springs of boiling bubbling water formed over 300 000 years ago. The site claims to be the world's only drive-in volcano and attracts a steady stream of visitors. Future plans may see the further development of the Soufrière area. In the past sulphur was mined here and currently the area is being explored as a source of geothermal energy.

Photo 19: The Pitons and Soufrière

Looking south from on the west coast, the town of Soufrière lies on flat land adjacent to the sea. It is surrounded by gently sloping, wooded hillsides and overlooked by the twin peaks of Gros Piton (798m) and Petit Piton (750m). The Pitons are the result of volcanic activity some 40 000 years ago, and are perhaps the island's most famous landmarks. The Soufrière/Canaries area has a population of about 10 000, and though popular with day visitors, offers only 3 per cent of the island's tourist accommodation. The town with its hot springs and volcano, is a major destination for many of the tour buses.

Photo 20: Sunset at Marigot

Marigot Bay just south of Castries bay has an inner and outer bay. Historically it is associated with the British success in taking control of the island from the French in 1778 in the Battle of Cul de Sac. The bay is considered one of the safest harbours from hurricanes in the Caribbean. It has a large yacht club and some hotel accommodation. It was also the setting for the film Doctor Dolittle with Rex Harrison. This breathtaking picture was taken at dusk, and shows one of the reasons why tourists come to St Lucia.

Banana landscapes

Photo 21: Banana-growing

The sugar estates which covered this part of St Lucia were bought by the Van Geest family in 1961 and transferred to banana production. In the Roseau valley south of Castries, banana cultivation occupies the flattest and most fertile area. Several roads running through the banana groves can be seen. A Windward Island Banana Grower's Association (WINBAN) research station is also visible in the background.

Photo 22: Harvesting hands of bananas, Dennery Farmco

Skilled cutters (men) select and 'de-hand' bunches into hands of 14-18 bananas using razor-sharp cutlasses. Careful selecting and culling ensures that the bananas are fully-grown and free from bruising. Each tree produces one crop but the tropical climate allows harvesting throughout the year.

Photo 23: Banana split

After cutting, the hands are laid on a banana leaf on the ground. Latex from the crown (where the bunch was cut) runs down the middle channel of the leaf, so the bananas are undamaged. After ten minutes, women carry the bananas on trays to the packing stations (at Dennery Farmco). Blue plastic sleeving covers the bananas on the tree to reduce moisture loss, to help the fruits form and to prevent insect and wind damage. Twine gives the trees support.

Photo 24: Field packing station, Dennery Farmco

Dennery Farmco on the east coast of St Lucia has 82 packing stations, located on the many feeder roads inside the estate. These women are dipping bananas into fungicide before packing them in boxes in prevent physical damage and fungus from spoiling the appearance of the fruit. The boxes in which the bananas are shipped around the world are visible. The general manager of the estate, Percy Combie, can be seen in the middle.

Photo 25: Workers carrying mangoes, Dennery Farmco

Head porterage is used to transport crops short distances. The feeder roads have been built on the routes followed by the rail lines on the old sugar plantations. Boxed bananas are collected from the field packing stations (photo 24) by tractor or lorry and taken to Castries or Vieux Fort. In this photo, mango trees can be seen to the left of the road, and a drainage ditch to the right.

Photo 26: Castries harbour — a link to the world

Every week throughout the year, on Wednesdays and Thursdays, long queues of trucks heavily laden with bananas inch slowly towards the checking and storage depots at the dockside in Castries harbour. The Geest Company buy the bananas from all St Lucia's farmers, then transfer them quickly to the refrigerated holds of the Geestline vessel which calls weekly at Castries *en route* to the UK, where the bananas are distributed to shops nationwide.

Photo 27: Bananas in the rain, Dennery Farmco

Bananas require high levels of rainfall (800mm) as well as high year-round temperatures (26°C). St Lucia has a tropical climate, with rain frequently falling in short but heavy showers, like the one shown in the photo. The road (centre) connects Dennery with Castries. In the fields where bananas are growing, the taller trees are coconut trees which have been 'intercropped' among the bananas to provide the farm with another crop for sale.

Photo 28: Planting pineapples, Mabouya Valley

A recent programme of crop diversification on Dennery Farmco involved cultivating 4.5ha with pineapples. 50 000 pineapple crowns (like those in the sacks) cost EC$36 000 (approximately £9000). After a good first crop, the pineapple bushes became infested with mealie bugs. Pineapple crowns are shown being replanted after fungicide and pesticide treatment. Women workers are overseen by a male agricultural manager from Trinidad.

6 Activity suggestions

These activities could form part of a study of a locality in the Caribbean or they could be integrated into thematic geography, ensuring that the locality is revisited on a number of occasions and approached from different perspectives. In either case integration of the skills, places and themes of geography will take place.

The aim of the activities is to enable children to investigate the following key questions:

- What is it like to live in Castries?
- Why has this part of St Lucia developed in this way?
- Why is St Lucia a special place?
- How is this locality linked with other parts of St Lucia and the rest of the world?
- How is St Lucia changing and why?
- What do different people think about the changes?
- Should St Lucia be like this and what should it be like in the future?

The geography National Curriculum requires an enquiry approach, so each activity has a question on which enquiry can be focused. Completion of all the activities should enable children to address all the above questions. Teacher assessment may be carried out by observation or by means of evidence produced by the children. For some activities groups of children will need to handle the pictures, for others some or all of the pictures should be prominently displayed. One photopack is adequate for all the activities, but some teachers might find the purchase of extra packs an advantage if larger numbers of children are required to do the activities simultaneously.

If a locality study is to be undertaken the familiarisation exercise should be carried out first as all the pictures will be in use. Subsequently the activities can take place in any order. For use in thematic geography topics a limited number of pictures will be introduced on each occasion so the familiarisation exercise may be dispensed with if so desired. Geographical enquiry gives many opportunities for the development of information technology skills. For instance where captions and titles are prepared for wall display, these may be prepared by means of word processing or desk top publishing techniques. Where data is collected, for instance concerning features which are like/unlike the home locality, the development of a simple database would be appropriate. A bank of St Lucian geographical vocabulary (like that on page 44) could also be developed using IT. Comparisons of weather data could make use of a simple graphing package.

Activities for key stage 1 (reception and years 1 and 2)

Activity 1: Main features

Photos:	8 and 19
Grouping:	whole class or groups in turn with teacher
Enquiry focus:	What would you see in St Lucia?

1 Discuss photo 8, examining physical features such as sea, forests, hills, mountain peaks, unfamiliar plants.

2 Examine photo 19 first for features similar to photo 8, such as hills, forest and sea. Then look for additional human features such as ships and boats, warehouses, containers, cranes, government office blocks, satellite dish.

3 What can you deduce from the photos about the weather (it is very hot and very wet), about the people (there are many of them living in towns) and about links with other places (trade goes on using ships and containers)?

Activity 2: Similarities and differences

Photos:	1, 2, 4 and 5; 3 and 6; 9 and 10
Grouping:	divide class into three groups (each with a helper if possible or teacher to take each group in turn). Groups must investigate each set of photos. Whole class for emphasis on similarities (photo 4)
Enquiry focus:	How is St Lucia like our place? How is it different?

1 Using the family photos name the children Hayle, Evvery, Thia and Gimel. Who is the eldest, the youngest, the only boy? Examine their clothes and school uniform. What does this tell you about the weather? What can you tell about the house, its building materials, and the garden? Make comparisons with own families and homes.

2 Use the school photos to examine the building, class size, lack of dividing walls between classes, desks, use of chalkboard. How do these compare with our school?

3 Look at the street photos and examine houses, shops, streets, cars, deep gutters (for storm water) and compare with local features.

4 Stress similarities. We all need homes, places to obtain food, places to learn and means of transport.

Activity 3: Effects of weather

Photos:	17, 20 and 27
Additional resources:	tourist literature and photos
Groupings:	whole class or groups in rotation with teacher
Enquiry focus:	What is the weather like and how does it affect people?

1 Look for weather evidence in the three photos and tourist literature.

2 Is the weather always the same (temperature and humidity are fairly constant) or does it vary from day to day (very little) from season to season (only in respect to the danger from hurricanes and tropical storms from August to November)?

3 Talk about the effect of weather on the growth of plants and trees, on the homes people build, on clothes, on roads and unsurfaced tracks.

4 Consider why people from the UK like to go to St Lucia on holiday, particularly in January and February. Does the weather affect their choice of a holiday place?

Activity 4: Use of land and buildings

Photos:	whole set displayed around the classroom
Grouping:	individuals should be free to move about to select photos to show to the rest of the class
Enquiry focus:	What do they use buildings for in St Lucia and what do they use land for?

1 Ask individuals to find the photos which show homes (1, 5, 8, 9, 10, 11, 12 and 19). Discuss where these homes are built, on flat land or hillsides.

2 Ask pupils to find school pictures (photos 3 and 6) and other public buildings, a church (4), health centre (7), port and government buildings (8), shops (10), a hotel (14), a factory (15). What other buildings might they find in Castries? (For example, fire station, post office, banks, university, airport terminal.)

3 Select photos which show use of land for farming (21-25, 27 and 28), trade with other places (8, 10, 13 and 26), fishing (16). What other uses of land might there be? (Roads, airports, port, forest for water catchment, golf course, factory estate.)

Activities for lower key stage 2 (years 3 and 4)

Activity 5: Familiarisation

Photos:	all or as many as desired
Grouping:	divide class into groups of three or four pupils
Enquiry focus:	What is it like in St Lucia?

1 Each group studies a different photo and then describes it to the rest of the class, with teacher intervention where appropriate.

2 A caption is suggested by the group, refined by the rest of the class and displayed with the photo.

3 The activity should be repeated ad lib, perhaps over several days.

Activity 6: Family

Photos:	1, 2, 4 and 5
Additional resources:	Hayle Harvey's story **Growing up in Castries** (pages 22-28)
Grouping:	whole class
Enquiry focus:	What is it like to be a child growing up in St Lucia?

1 Read Hayle Harvey's story 'Growing up in Castries', in its entirety or the extracts referring to her family.

2 Identify the members of the family. Display the photos and label them.

3 Enlarge and display Gimel and Thia's self portraits from **Growing up in Castries**. Children draw their own self portraits.

4 Spot the similarities/differences between the Harveys' locality and own locality. List and display.

5 Start collecting new (geographical) words and display them.

Activity 7: Homes

Photos:	1, 5, 8, 9, 10, 11 and 12
Grouping:	class divided into seven groups
Enquiry focus:	What are homes like in St Lucia?

1 In seven groups examine one photo of St Lucia and extract information about a home or homes in it. Discuss in group.

2 Teacher questions class, individuals answering using evidence from own photo:
   a are they made of wood/brick/concrete or what?
   b are the roofs tiles/corrugated iron or what?
   c are the windows glass/covered by venetian blinds or what?
   d are they bigger/smaller than ... (known building)?
   e are there verandas, if so why?
   f do the houses stand on stilts, if so why?
   g are the homes separated/grouped together/isolated?
   h are all the homes the same in type/size/situation/building materials?

3 Draw conclusions from the discussion and summarise in wall display:
   - Homes in St Lucia are like ours because ...
   - Homes in St Lucia are different from ours because ...

   Add drawings of own homes and St Lucian homes.

Activity 8: School

Photos:	2, 6 and 7
Grouping:	divide class into group of fours or less
Enquiry focus:	What is it like to go to school in St Lucia?

1 Agree by discussion some of the features of a school:
   a children, teachers other adults;
   b buildings, classrooms, playground, field;
   c lessons, books, displays, PE and games, food;
   d a place to go if you are unwell.

2 Rotate the three photos around the groups asking children to identify equivalent features. Meanwhile other groups draw a range of features of their own school.

3 Class discussion on what is different, what is the same. Display findings and drawings under the headings:
   - Gimel's school is like ours because .....
   - Gimel's school is different from ours because .....

Activity 9: Weather

Photos:	1, 6, 7, 8, 9, 11, 16, 17, 19 and 20-28
Additional resources:	Hayle Harvey's story **Growing up in Castries**. Caribbean tourist literature. Weather and climate statistics
Grouping:	whole class
Enquiry focus:	What is the weather like in St Lucia?

1 Display all appropriate photos and ask children to find visual clues about St Lucia's weather.
2 Children propose statements with evidence from a particular photo.
3 Collect and summarise statements (should include high temperatures all year, very heavy rainfall particularly from August to October and over high ground.)
4 Read Hayle Harvey's account of Hurricane Allen.
5 Display tourist literature for the Caribbean. Consider whether it truly represents local weather conditions.
6 Make collage representation of rainforest, tourist beaches and hurricane devastation.
7 Compare climate statistics with local figures.

Activity 10: Water

Photos:	8, 9, 10, 12, 16, 17, 19, 20, 26 and 27
Additional resources:	weather and climate statistics. Ordnance Survey map of St Lucia
Grouping:	groups of four/five each group to take turns
Enquiry focus:	Where do you find water in St Lucia's natural environment? Are some parts of St Lucia nicer than others?

1 Display appropriate photos asking children for evidence of high rainfall.
2 Collect, summarise and display findings (should include overhanging roofs, deep road drains, partially water eroded road surface, heavy shower in photo 27, lush vegetation).
3 Let children find the river photo (12) and locate Castries river on street map (recent low rainfall has cause the river to dry up).
4 Let children identify all the sea photos (8, 16, 19, 20 and 26) and locate on St Lucia map or Ordnance Survey map if available.
5 Display the river and sea photos only and encourage the children to consider which would be pleasant and/or interesting places to visit. Encourage independent choices and avoid influence by implication.
6 Using counters or cubes in different colours the children vote for their three favourites in order of preference. Make a block graph of the results, using suitable software or a wall chart.
7 Discuss why some ties are more desirable than others. Consider ways in which the unpopular sites might be improved.

Activity 11: Journeys

Photos:	2, 7-10, 13, 16, 17, 20, 21 and 26
Additional resources:	enlarged maps, Ordnance Survey map of St Lucia, world map and globe, Caribbean tourist literature, Hayle Harvey's story **Growing up in Castries**
Grouping:	groups of three/four with free access to all resources
Enquiry focus:	How and why do people make journeys around and to St Lucia?

1 Devise questions about journeys around Castries, eg. how do you get from the Anglican Infant School to the Health Centre/library/market/fire station? Encourage answers which:
   a use the shortest route;
   b use directions, left and right;
   c use the alpha/numeric grid, always quoting the horizontal axis before the vertical (eg. the school is in K5).

2 Display all relevant photos. Discuss how people travel around St Lucia, what forms of transport are used? (Find evidence of cars, minibuses, trucks, pick ups, lorries, road surface, boats, walking.)

3 Work out distances compared with local journeys. For example, how far is it for the Harvey family to go by car from Mon Giraud to:
   a Castries for work and school;
   b Laborie to visit grandfather;
   c Choiseul to visit grandmother.

4 If the road surfaces are like that shown in photo 17 what effect will this have on journey time? (St Lucian journeys probably take twice as long as those on rural roads in the UK.)

5 Bananas grown at Dennery Farmco are transported to Castries and Vieux Fort to be loaded on the Geest ship. How far and how long might these journeys take?

6 Rawle Harvey flies a light aeroplane.
   - Where are the two places where he could land on the island?
   - Where does he probably keep the plane?
   - Which other islands do they probably visit? (See Hayle Harvey's story **Growing up in Castries**.)

7 Using tourist literature, a world map and a globe, work out how tourists reach St Lucia from the UK, other European countries and the USA.

8 Cruise liners call at Castries, so use maps of the Caribbean to plan cruises which visit many interesting places. Work out how long such cruises might take.

Activity 12: People at work

Photos:	7, 13-15 and 21-28
Additional resources:	*World Studies 8-13* (Simon Fisher and David Hicks, Oliver and Boyd, 1985)
Grouping:	divide class into four groups or as appropriate for role play
Enquiry focus:	What sort of work do people do on St Lucia?

1 Display photos 7, 13, 14 and 15 and identify type of work going on in each. Consider lifestyles, journeys and types of work involved.

2 Develop work situations in group role play, with teacher intervention to increase understanding. Act out to the rest of the class:
   a child brought into health centre after playground accident;
   b market stallholder collecting up goods, family and takings at the end of the day;
   c security guard warning off teenagers trespassing at a hotel;
   d woman factory worker discussing work and family matters with friends during lunch break.

3 Display photos 21-28, the agricultural sequence. Identify different jobs represented:

• planters • cutters • packers • estate manager • agricultural manager

Consider other work implied in the process of banana/other fruit production:

• planting • spraying with insecticide • protecting with plastic bags • supporting trees with twine • packing lorries and trucks • driving to the port • checking quality • weighing fruit and paying farmers • loading the ship • sailing the ship to Barry in South Wales

Allot jobs to individuals or groups who act their part of the process in sequence. Dockers, drivers and retailers in the UK can be added if desired. A financial dimension stressing inequalities of international trade can be added by reference to 'The Journey of Bananas' and the 'Return of the Pennies' in *World Studies 8-13*.

4 Consider evidence from the photos and text of the different jobs undertaken by men and women. Should they necessarily be gender related?

Activity 13: Landscapes	
Photos:	8, 12 and 17-21
Additional resources:	Castries map, St Lucia map
Grouping:	whole class for 1 and 2 (ongoing), six groups in rotation for 3-8
Enquiry focus:	What is the landscape of St Lucia like?

1 Identify the following in the photos and locate them on the St Lucia map:
- volcanic activity (the Sulphur Springs),
- extinct volcanic cones (the Pitons),
- part of a river (Castries River),
- a large bay (Castries Harbour),
- a small sheltered bay (Marigot Harbour),
- a flat plain (Roseau plantation).

2 Collect new geographical vocabulary.

3 Use photo 8 and the Castries map to consider why the town is sited here (large natural harbour on the sheltered side of the island, flat surrounding land.)
- Why is the large warehouse sited thus? (Access to deep water berths.)
- Why are the new government buildings thus sited? (Prestigious waterfront site in capital city, impressive to visitors.)

4 What has caused the damage in photo 12 (rubbish, effluents) and in photo 17 (overuse, weathering, poor maintenance)?

5 The Sulphur Springs at Soufrière attract many visitors. Consider who might want to visit this site. (School pupils and their teachers, tourists, scientists.)

6 Study photo 19 and the map of St Lucia. Consider why Soufrière is thus sited. (Natural bay on the sheltered side of the island, flat land, near to the Pitons — much beloved symbol of the country.)

7 Locate Marigot Harbour (photo 20) on the map and consider why it is safe from hurricanes.

8 Why is Roseau (photo 21) the ideal banana plantation on St Lucia?

Activities for upper key stage 2 (years 5 and 6)

All the earlier activities can be made more demanding for older children by requiring logical, well argued, written responses from individuals. This should always be preceded by the collaborative groupwork previously suggested.

The following additional questions could form the focus for enquiry at this stage:

- Which physical and human features in and around Castries make this locality distinctive?
- What are the reasons for the similarities and differences when compared with the home area?
- How are people using or modifying the environments of St Lucia?
- What are the local views and our views of these changes?
- How are the occupations, land use and settlement patterns in and around Castries related to its environment and location?

St Lucia: a geographical vocabulary

agriculture	jetty
airport	latex
Arawak	market
bananas	moist
Carib	mountain
Caribbean Sea	nature reserve
climate	package tour
conservation	plantation
crop	port
cruise ship	rainforest
cutlass	ripen
estate	sucker
fertile	timber
fishing	tourist
harbour	tropical storm
humid	volcano
industry	waterfall

Activity 14: Work and Leisure	
Photos:	all
Additional resources:	material from the St Lucia Tourist Board
Grouping:	whole class for 1, groups of three/four for 2-7
Enquiry focus:	How do work and leisure activities in the Castries area compare with our own?

1 Pupils select all photos giving evidence of or implying paid employment.

2 Consider the necessary skills and training required by: the teacher, the journalist (Hayle), the refrigeration/air conditioning specialist (Rawle), the nurse, the mini-bus driver, the government office worker, the docker, the shopkeeper, the artist (who is uncle to the Harvey children), the market trader, the hotel receptionist, the factory worker, the fisherman, the banana cutter, banana packers, the banana estate manager, the pineapple planters, the agricultural manager.

3 Categorise jobs likely to be available under the following headings:
   a for girls/boys leaving school before 16;
   b for girls/boys leaving secondary school at 16;
   c for girls/boys qualifying at the College in Castries/University in the West Indies.
   Are the divisions between women's and men's work valid? What could be done to make opportunities more equal?
   Compare job opportunities in Castries with your own local area.

4 One village school in St Lucia has this motto: 'Learn now to earn later'. Invent some mottos to encourage:
   a children to work hard at school;
   b parents to support higher education of girls;
   c employers to give fair wages to both men and women.

5 Put photos 21-26 in sequence and consider the process of banana production and marketing (ensure that the photos are previously mixed up and identification numbers are covered.)

6 The scene in photo 25 was previously part of a sugar plantation, with slave labour and a railway system instead of roads. There are fears that the European Single Market may damage the banana trade. What might replace this scene in 50/100 years time? (Diversified tropical fruit farming, eroded barren landscape and a tourist playground.)

7 You are staying at the Royal St Lucian Hotel for two weeks. Plan some visits that you would like to make and work out itineraries for them. You may hire a self drive car or a mini bus and driver by the day. Plan activities for each day of the holiday. (Use literature from the St Lucian Tourist Board if available.) Compare this holiday with the equivalent in a resort in the UK.

Activity 15: Town and country

Photos:	all
Additional resources:	St Lucia map (copies for each group if possible). Ordnance Survey map of St Lucia if available
Grouping:	groups of no more than four
Enquiry focus:	What differences are there between town and country life in St Lucia, compared with the UK?

1 St Lucians categorise their settlements thus:

a Castries the capital city;
b Soufrière, Vieux Fort and Gros Islet as towns;
c Laborie, Choiseul, Canaries, Anse la Raye, Dennery and Micoud as villages.

There are also ten districts or parishes most of which take their names from towns or villages.

One group should locate all the photos within these categories:

• city • town • village • other

The other groups, unaware of the St Lucian definitions, should choose categories and distinguish the photos according to their own perception of town and country.

Compare the St Lucian perception of town/village and our own.

2 Debate the rival attractions of town and country, giving examples of St Lucia and the UK.

3 Choose a favourite photo. Discuss likes and dislikes.

4 Choose appropriate sites for the following:

a a teaching hospital specialising in tropical diseases and serving all of the Windward Islands;
b an experimental farm developing a wide variety of exotic fruits for the world market;
c a wildlife park conserving the plants and animals of St Lucia;
d a luxury hideaway for a multi-millionaire.

Activity 16: Change

Photos:	all
Additional resources:	access to all available
Grouping:	prepare in groups of five/six and present to class. Final activity individually
Enquiry focus:	What changes are occurring on St Lucia? What do the local people think about them? What is my view?

1 A luxury hotel has been built at Jalousie between the Pitons, a site of great emotional importance to St Lucians. Such developments promote conflicting views.
   a Tourism brings money and employment to the local area.
   b Rainforest has been cleared, destroying wildlife habitats.
   c Buildings are camouflaged to blend into the landscape.
   d Excavations have damaged beaches, coral reefs and pre-Columbian antiquities.
   e Road access will benefit locals as well as tourists.
   f Surplus vegetables grown on site will affect local smallholders' trade.

   Debate the case for such a development from the point of view of a young school leaver in Soufrière, a conservationist, a government minister seeking re-election, a construction worker who worked on the site but who is now out of work. Write headlines and newspaper accounts of public meetings where these views have been aired.

2 You are preparing brochures to encourage:
   a young people to live and work in rural areas;
   b overseas investors to set up factories in St Lucia;
   c Europeans to visit St Lucia on holiday.

   Which photos would you select to illustrate each brochure? Provide three reasons to justify your choice.

3 What changes would you suggest to improve the environments shown in photo 12 (Castries river), photo 17, (road surface) and one of your own choice? If such changes were made who would they affect in the short/long term? What different views might you encounter? Can you still justify your improvements?

4 Choose three photos showing relatively undeveloped parts of St Lucia. How might these places change if ...
   a tourist hotels and associated facilities trebled in the next few years;
   b all St Lucian families owned cars;
   c banana growing collapsed and investment in manufacturing trebled?

5 Choose photos of people and suggest what they might think about such issues as:
   - secondary schooling for all;
   - fair wages for fair work;
   - equal opportunities for girls and boys;
   - new hotel developments;
   - conservation of wildlife and historic sites.

Activity 17: Summary

Photos:	all
Additional resources:	any available
Grouping:	divide class into groups of four/five for 1, individual responses to 2, whole class for 3
Enquiry focus:	How do St Lucians make use of their environment?

1 Analyse the positive and negative points about life in St Lucia under the following headings:
- lifestyle
- homes
- schools
- work
- landscapes and environment
- weather and climate
- communications and transport
- tourism

2 Summarise all you know about the St Lucians' use of their environment in a written account under these paragraph headings:
a Where in the world is St Lucia?
b Growing up in town and country.
c Different kinds of work.
d Environment in danger.
e Changes for the better or worse?

3 Use the above in conjunction with the photos to make a display about St Lucia to show to teachers, other pupils and parents.

7 Resources and further information

Some of the resources listed here focus specifically on St Lucia, others contain information about aspects of the Caribbean lifestyle and economy in general.

Publications

Two special issues of *Primary Geographer*, the Geographical Association's magazine for primary teachers, are devoted to St Lucia. Photos, maps (at different scales), cartoons and statistics are included in each issue with a variety of activity suggestions.

1 *Primary Geographer* number 9 (April 1992) deals with teaching about a locality in an economically developing country, using Castries in St Lucia as an example. 16 pages, packed with information and resources about growing up in St Lucia; the island's environments, weather, farming and industry; and recent developments.
The Geographical Association, 1992.

2 *Primary Geographer* number 22 (July 1995) comprises 32 pages of new material on St Lucia, including an update on the Harvey family, details of tropical storm Debbie and an environmental game. There is also a story and music from St Lucia.
The Geographical Association, 1995.

Lessons on Castries, St Lucia
Wendy Morgan
This 48-page book maximises the use of all the available resources on St Lucia, and its 20 lesson plans are designed to deliver a significant component of the key stage 2 geography curriculum. It offers imaginative activities and investigations by 'taking' the pupils on a 'visit' to St Lucia with opportunities for studying the climate and weather, the island's flora and fauna, the islanders' viewpoints and lifestyles and the impact of tourism.
The Geographical Association, 1994.

Cambridge Primary Geography: Living in St Lucia
Vincent Bunce and Wendy Morgan
The set comprises:

1 Twelve A3 full colour laminated photocards each presenting an image of one aspect of life in St Lucia, plus one of a picture-map. The back of each card contains key questions, a glossary, descriptive text and a range of activities.

2 A pupil's book which has been written for use at key stage 2 and explores St Lucia through the eyes of the Harvey family. Each section comprises one topic which focuses on a key question.

3 A teacher's resource book with background notes, commentary on pages in the pupil's book and 30 photocopiable activity sheets.

Cambridge University Press, 1996.

My Grandpa and the Sea
Katherine Orr
A charming story about the relationship between a young girl growing up on the Island of St Lucia and her grandfather. The story focuses on grandfather's life as a fisherman and on the changes he faces as his industry develops. A strong environmental theme runs through the story, which is illustrated in colour.
Carolrhoda Books Inc., Minneapolis, 1990.
Available from Worldaware.

Images of Earth: a teacher's guide to remote sensing in geography at key stage 2
Edited by Michael Barnett, Ashley Kent and Mike Milton
This pack has general information about using remotely-sensed images with key stage 2 pupils. It also includes maps, aerial photographs, satellite images, notes and activities specifically about St Lucia.
The Geographical Association, 1994.

The Banana Education Pack
A cross-curricular project pack for key stage 2 which looks at the origins and cultivation of bananas and nutrition issues. Includes several activity sheets.
Educational Project Resources.
One pack per school is available free from EPR (address below).

The Caribbean: Making Our Own Choices
Neil Macdonald
A useful background text for teachers which examines development throughout the Caribbean. Accounts of Oxfam-supported community development projects are interspersed with poems, songs, photos and case studies which set the projects in their social, economic and environmental context.
Oxfam, 1990.

Go Bananas
A photo-based activity pack for key stages 2/3 focusing on the journey of a banana from being planted in the Caribbean (St Vincent) to being sold and eaten in the UK. Contains 18 black and white photos, maps and teacher's guide with activity suggestions.
Oxfam, 1990.

Maps

Satellite map: St Lucia
A poster-sized (765 x 570mm) satellite image in full colour. This was taken from 832km and introduces pupils to the exciting world of images from space. The image allows settlements, vegetation and other geographical features to be easily identified. Includes activity ideas for teachers, related to National Curriculum geography.
Worldaware, 1992.

Ordnance Survey Worldmap 4: St Lucia
A 1:50 000 map of St Lucia with an inset map of Castries.
Ordnance Survey, 1991.
Available from the GA and approved Ordnance Survey stockists.

St Lucia Mapcard
An A4 full-colour glossy map of St Lucia illustrating the island's main physical and human features. The card also provides pupils with some basic information about St Lucia including farming, population, transport and communications. Printed on card and laminated.
Worldaware, 1994.

Caribbean map
This new map is ideal as a classroom resource. Includes insets of Guyana and a world map showing the region's geographical location.
Oxfam, 1992.

Audio and visual resources

BBC Radio: Notes on Castries, St Lucia
Ten 15-minute BBC radio programmes. Each investigates one aspect of St Lucian life, and include: A family at home; Going to school; Weather, climate and landscape; Travelling around the island; Visiting places of interest; Work on a banana plantation.
BBC Radio, 1993.
Copies of the programmes are available from the London Borough of Richmond's 'Young People's Services' (address below).

St Lucia slide show and lecture for schools.
Contact: Mike Howarth (address below).

Slide sets

1 *At Home in St Lucia*
Twelve colour slides with notes about the Harvey family. This family, also the focus of other classroom material about St Lucia, are featured at home, work, school and play as they go about their everyday lives.
Worldaware, 1993.

2 *Banana Landscapes*
A set of twelve colour slides with notes focusing on aspects of agriculture in St Lucia. The cultivation of bananas is examined in detail, from the banana tree in the field, through the washing and packing processes and to the port.
Worldaware, 1993.

3 *Connexions*
Twelve colour slides with notes focusing on transport and communications, this set looks at transport on the island as well as links with the outside world, and helps to answer the question 'How is this place connected to other places?'.
Worldaware, 1992.

Video Penpals: St Lucia
A 15-minute video showing what it is like to grow up in St Lucia. The film focuses on the lives of children living in Soufriere. The children are pictured at home and school, talking about their homes, families and lives.
Channel 4 Television
Available from Worldaware.

Whose Place? St Lucia
This 15-minute video presents a vivid picture of St Lucia's environment and the types of work available to its inhabitants. It examines the choices which face the island as it considers how best to develop. We meet four islanders — André, a diver; Paul, a banana grower; Beverly, a factory worker; and Walter, a hotel employee, and explore St Lucia's future through their eyes, and consider how different types of development will affect them as well as the island.
Carlton UK Television.
Available from Worldaware.

Our Place: The Harveys in St Lucia
A 20-minute video which portrays daily life for the Harvey family. This video shows members of the Harvey family talking about their daily lives. It also follows them to school and work, and shows them shopping and relaxing at home. The film offers insights into St Lucia's geography and environment.
Carlton UK Television.
Available from Worldaware.

Software

Distant Places
This CD-Rom includes a section on St Lucia.
Available from The Advisory Unit for Computers in Education (address below).

Addresses and useful contacts

The Advisory Unit for Computers in Education, 126 Great North Road, Hatfield, Hertfordshire AL9 5JZ.

Cambridge University Press, The Edinburgh Building, Shaftesbury Road, Cambridge CB2 2RU.

The Commonwealth Institute has a permanent display on the Caribbean, and offers occasional INSET for teachers wanting to learn about St Lucia. Address: Kensington High Street, London W8 6NQ.
Tel: 0171 603 4535.

Development Education Association, Third Floor, 29-31 Cowper Street, London EC2A 4AP.

Educational Project Resources, Banana Education Services, Freepost, London SW7 4YY. Tel: 0171 373 7716.

The Geographical Association, 343 Fulwood Road, Sheffield S10 3BP.
Tel: 0114 267 0666. Fax: 0114 267 0688.

Mike Howarth, 47 West Hill, Hitchin, Hertfordshire SG5 2HY.

The Latin American Bureau provide a useful Caribbean resource list for teachers.
Address: 1 Amwell Street, London EC1R 1UL.

London Borough of Richmond's 'Young People's Services', The Cottage, Little Green, Richmond TW9 1QL. Tel: 0181 940 0590.
Contact: Ms Tricia Hebblethwaite.

For school links with St Lucia contact: The Ministry of Education and Culture (Primary), Castries, St Lucia, West Indies.

Oxfam (Education), 274 Banbury Road, Oxford OX2 7DZ. Tel: 01865 311311.

The St Lucia Tourist Board can provide information about tourism in St Lucia.
Address: 421a Finchley Road, London NW3 6HJ. Tel: 0171 431 3675.

Worldaware, 31-35 Kirby Street, London EC1N 8TE. Tel: 0171 831 3844.
Fax: 0171 831 1746.